P9-EMK-439

FRONTIER PRESIDENT:

James K. Polk

FRONTIER PRESIDENT:

James K. Polk

By BILL SEVERN

IVES WASHBURN, INC. · NEW YORK

FRONTIER PRESIDENT: JAMES K. POLK

LIBRARY OF CONGRESS CATALOG CARD NUMBER: 65-12069

MANUFACTURED IN THE UNITED STATES OF AMERICA

Chapter One

HARDLY ANYBODY thought little Jimmy Polk would ever amount to much. He was Sam Polk's oldest son and the Polks had always been leaders in Mecklenburg County, North Carolina, but Jimmy was a small and rather sickly boy, shy and bashful, a quiet one. Everybody agreed he was a good boy who tried hard to do what was expected of him, but the general opinion was that he would need all the advantages his family could give him. He lacked the physical strength a boy needed in that time and place and while he was far from stupid, he never said or did anything to make folks think he was very smart.

But he had another strength that grew from the land and the people, from the books he later learned to use, and maybe from his own need to make the very most of talents considered only average. More than anything, he had courage. His body never grew strong and he was seldom in really good health, but when he set his mind on doing something, there was nothing that could keep him from it. There were few tasks he undertook that he ever left unfinished.

As a boy, he lived in the shadow of the stronger and bolder ones and as a man, there were others who captured more popular attention. But while they were talking, he was doing. For fourteen years, he helped shape the laws of the nation in Congress, twice served as Speaker of the House, was Governor of Tennessee, and became the President who made a continental nation of the United States.

Just as the earlier Polks helped to stretch the frontiers, he stretched the office of the Presidency to new dimensions, and in doing so, completed the annexation of Texas, settled the Oregon border dispute, actively commanded the Mexican War, and added to America all the rich lands that later became the far western states. He announced at the start of his Presidential term exactly what he meant to do and, within four years, did what he had promised.

When he was born in 1795, the heroes of the American Revolution were still among the living and there were still Indians to be seen in the woods around his father's farm. If the days of fighting the redskins were over, just as the years of battling the British redcoats were, the spirit of the pioneers was much alive. He learned about the struggle of settling the land from those who had been through it, and of the battles for liberty and independence from those who had fought them. His own family was a living legend of the pioneers.

The Polks were among minor royalty back in Scotland where the family name began as Pollock. When a branch of the family moved to estates in Ireland, the way of saying the name gradually changed to Polk. Setting out for the New World, Polks became among the early settlers of Maryland's Eastern Shore. One of the Marylanders, William Polk, took his family to Pennsylvania's Cumberland Valley. When his son, Thomas, came of an age to want a farm of his own, he sought another frontier. Thomas led the way through the Virginia Valley and beyond all the settlements into North Carolina in 1753. In the fertile country near the southern border of the province, he cleared the land and built one of the first cabins on Sugar Creek.

The rest of the family and some of their neighbors made the difficult journey from Pennsylvania to join him there. Among them was his youngest brother, six-year-old Ezekiel, whom Thomas took into his household after their father died. Gradually the wilderness gave way to crops that flourished in the red clay soil and to the building of more log cabins. The best lands belonged to the Polks who had come to them first. But even before all the lands along Sugar Creek were cleared, the sturdy Scotch-Irish pioneers built rough log preaching stands in the woods to hold worship according to the strict faith of their religion. Within a few years, they had put up the first Presbyterian meeting houses that became the centers of their community life.

The Polks and their friends at first supported the orderly government of the Crown and the British governor of the province, William Tryon. As Sugar Creek's leading citizen and a man who had become powerful throughout the province, Thomas Polk promoted the setting up of the new county of Mecklenburg and became one of its magistrates. He sponsored the county seat town of Charlotte and was a captain of the militia and a delegate to the provincial assembly. Meanwhile, he did what he could to help his younger brother, Ezekiel, follow in his footsteps.

But Ezekiel was more of a rebel than the prospering Thomas. There was a restlessness in him and a stubborn streak of independence, a hard-minded will to do things his own way. As a youth, growing up in the comparative luxury of his brother's home, he seemed only interested in having a good time. Thomas provided well for him and gave him a good education, but Ezekiel just couldn't seem to settle down. He was quick-witted, a glib talker, a bold and charming young man who could sweep others to follow his enthusiasms, but often he was too impulsive to see things through. When Ezekiel was in his twenties, Thomas managed to have him appointed a court clerk of a boundary area across the river in South Carolina, a job that carried with it high political favors.

Ezekiel married Maria Wilson, daughter of a wealthy farmer, and established a large farm of his own. They soon had twins, a son and a daughter. His second son, Samuel, who was to become the father of the future President, was born there in 1772.

Thomas began to resent British interference in the affairs of the county and as talk of revolution grew throughout the colonies, he organized a secret group of patriots. When news from Massachusetts of the actual outbreak of war at Lexington and Concord reached Sugar Creek, he called a meeting on May 31, 1775. It created a revolutionary committee to take over county government and adopted the historic Mecklenburg Resolves, one of the first American declarations of independence from British rule. Thomas became a Revolutionary War colonel, one of his sons was a major, and two other Polk brothers saw action as captains of militia.

In nearby South Carolina, Ezekiel was as quick to join the patriots and was made captain of a mounted regiment. But even in war, he was a man who insisted on making his own decisions. As a result of refusing to obey orders that went against his ideas as to how the war should be fought, he came close to being charged with treason. Ezekiel moved his family back across the river to North Carolina to a farm he bought from Thomas on the east side of Sugar Creek about ten miles from Charlotte. While the war raged farther to the north, he put his whole effort into raising crops and adding to his land.

For a time, he also ran a tavern in Charlotte and was a justice of the peace. When the British again threatened the immediate area, he took to the field with the militia and made fiery patriotic speeches to arouse the citizenry. But once more, Ezekiel risked the condemnation of his neighbors by dealing with the enemy to protect property during the British occupation of Charlotte. Yet when the British were forced to withdraw, his services in the patriot cause restored him to his neighbors' good graces. Ezekiel was elected in 1782 to Mecklenburg's most important political office of sheriff. Three months later he resigned after a dispute over conditions at the jail.

With the war won, Ezekiel was restless for some new adventure and Thomas provided him with the opportunity. Through his growing political power in the state, Thomas became one of the leaders in a great land company partnership. It was organized to take advantage of legislation that threw open to settlement the huge North Carolina wilderness domain, including most of what was to become the state of Tennessee. The combine had advance knowledge of what was coming and put locators on the field long before anybody else. Thomas had Ezekiel chosen as one of the surveyors and promised him a vast tract of land as his reward for helping to set the boundaries.

Indian raids soon drove the surveyors out and Ezekiel had to come home again, but not before he had a good look at the rich new country. He bought the rights to lands he wanted, awaited his chance to return, and in 1790 secured another appointment as a surveyor and took his family from Sugar Creek on the long journey west over the mountains to settle. Ezekiel arrived just as the Southwest Territory was being organized and Governor William Blount, who had been associated with Thomas in the land partnerships, appointed Ezekiel one of the magistrates of the new county. But his fields had hardly been cleared for planting before Ezekiel was forced back to North Carolina for a second time. His wife, Maria, had become seriously ill and because he loved her, he gave up his new settlement in the Territory to take the family back to Mecklenburg where she could be among her friends. Despite his prayers for her recovery, she died that fall. A year later, Ezekiel married again.

Meanwhile, his son Sam was growing up, a sturdy, level-headed youth, far less impulsive in his ways than his father, but with a streak of the old man's independence. Ezekiel sent him to school in Charlotte, saw to it that he had a good start in the world, and on a visit to Hopewell in the northern part of Mecklenburg, Sam met and began courting Jane Knox. She was eighteen and Sam four years older and the fact that he was a Polk made him quite a catch for Jane. Her father, Captain James Knox, was a well-to-do farmer whose courage in leading a charge right up to the muzzle of a British cannon during the Battle of Hanging Rock had made him one of the local heroes of the Revolution. He was equally respected by the people of Hopewell as a pillar of the church.

Sam and Jane were almost ready to announce their wedding date when her father died. They waited ten weeks out of respect for him, but were too much in love to delay the ceremony longer. On Christmas night in 1794, they were married at the home of Jane's widowed mother and went to live on a 250-acre farm that Ezekiel presented to his son. It was on Sugar Creek, several miles south of his own plantation. Jane received the income from a fifth of her father's estate, plus a third of his household furniture, cows, calves, a mare and a feather bed, along with other gifts that got the couple started.

The following November, close to noon on the second day of the month, their first son was born and they named him, after her father, James Knox Polk. Jane chose the name, but Sam agreed that they couldn't have given the boy a better one. He took pride in it in later years as he learned the story of his namesake's heroism in the Revolution and in some ways he grew up to resemble him more than he did any of the Polks. But if the birth of a son brought joy into the lives of Sam Polk and his wife, the event soon brought trouble, too. The baby became the center of a controversy which shook the entire county and led to bitterness and arguments that went on around him all his early years.

Jane had been raised in a home where religion was the most important thing, schooled in the fixed doctrines of Presbyterianism, never questioning the absolute authority of the church over the lives of all the people of the county. Sam shared her religious beliefs up to a point, but he resented the attempt by some clergymen to dictate matters of politics and community affairs which he felt people should have the freedom to decide for themselves. Every Sunday before the baby was born, he took Jane the seven miles to services at the Providence meeting house. He had no liking, however, for the young parson, James Wallis, who ruled over the congregation with an iron hand. When the minister began to make some pointed remarks about religious indifference, which the whole congregation knew were directed at Sam, his resentment grew. Although he continued to go to church regularly with Jane, Wallis angered Sam so that he found it increasingly hard to hold his temper.

Because he loved his wife, he gave in to her wish to have the baby baptized at the meeting house. But when the parson refused to perform the ceremony unless Sam pledged his own complete faith and obedience, the two men had words. The argument between Sam and Parson Wallis exploded in a violent quarrel. Little Jimmy was taken home without being baptized. Not until he was close to death would he seek the baptism that was refused him that day.

However, it was Grandfather Ezekiel, not Sam, who carried on the fight. For him, it became a crusade, not merely to justify his son's action, but to attack the hold the church had on affairs of the community and to question the absolute doctrines of the faith. Ezekiel made himself a champion of free religious thought, organized debates from one end of the county to the other, and circulated a library of books that included Thomas Paine's *Age of Reason.*

Parson Wallis published pamphlets to answer Ezekiel's arguments, hit back at him in sermons, and was joined by other members of the clergy in what became a running battle that had the whole of Mecklenburg upset. Before it was over, it turned political, with Parson Wallis hinting that Ezekiel was involved in some mysterious plot to overthrow the federal government. The parson's charges managed to alarm President John Adams' administration so much that warnings were issued from Philadelphia and an attempt was made to put Ezekiel under arrest. The Presbyterians staged great revival meetings that attracted hundreds of people to demonstrate the strength of the faith.

For Jane Polk, torn between love for her husband and

the depth of her religious convictions, the years of quarreling were hard. It became worse when her widowed mother chose Parson Wallis' father for her second husband. The years were no less hard for Sam. He had never meant to start the furor that had come of his quarrel with the minister. He and Jane tried to shield little Jimmy from the storm of dispute that surrounded them. But there were bound to be things he overheard, questions he asked, conversations quickly hushed that puzzled and troubled him. In later years he seldom talked about his early boyhood.

Yet the farm itself was a happy place for a growing boy. He ran barefoot most of the time in the long warm days that kept him out-of-doors and he learned to ride a horse almost as soon as he could walk. Beyond the rich bottom lands where tobacco and later cotton grew, there was a creek in which he could splash around with the boys from neighboring farms, although he never did learn to swim. There were the woods to play in, simple chores to keep his hands busy, and now and then an exciting trip into the little town of Charlotte, or up the road to Grandfather Ezekiel's place.

Much of the time, he was left to himself and he learned self-reliance based on discovering his skills and thinking things out on his own. He found pleasure in simple things well-done, in his father's praise for a completed task, and in the reward of his mother's smile when he learned to recite the words of a psalm or to sing one of the hymns she taught him. In the winter evenings, he copied the letters of the alphabet she wrote on his slate and listened by the fireside as his father talked of the work in the fields. From them both, he learned the virtues of a plain and industrious way of life.

But it also was a life of plenty, without the hardships

some boys had. His home was made of hewn logs, but it was far from being a crude cabin. Better than most, it boasted all the comforts those years could offer. There were two buildings, each with its chimney, and a covered passageway that joined them. Like other well-to-do planters, his father had several slaves to work in the fields, and there were two house girls for his mother. Skirting the farm and leading across a bridge his father owned was the post road, used by mail carriers twice a week and by the wagons that hauled crops to market, so that the farm was not an isolated place.

There were books in his home, from which he learned to read with his mother's help. And his parents' talk wasn't all of crops or of the farm. For a woman of those times, his mother had more than the average interest in the world of ideas and especially in the political conflicts of the new federal government. His father, although less active in politics than most of the Polks, was deeply concerned with the affairs of the county because of his family's part in them.

Jefferson was their hero, and Jimmy's life-long belief in the Jeffersonian ideals of government began in those earliest years of first hearing his mother and father praise him. Most of Mecklenburg shared their feelings more deeply than merely by taking sides in political argument. Jefferson was the defender of their way of life, champion of the rights of the individual man, of the independent farmer, and of all they had fought for in the Revolution. Here, where the first resolves of independence had been made under the leadership of Jimmy's own relatives, the election of 1800 became a second war of liberty.

Jimmy was only five at the time Jefferson opposed Alexander Hamilton and the aristocratic bankers and merchants who supported the Federalist cause in that great battle for the Presidency. He was still too young to understand the issues involved, but his mother and father and all the older folks hardly talked of anything else and the reverence in which Jefferson was held made a lasting impression. He heard both his father and his Grandfather Ezekiel hotly denounce Cousin William Polk, the county's wealthiest man and also its leading Federalist, as a traitor to his family. And although he couldn't make sense of all that was said, he was old enough to know Tom Jefferson seemed to be the hero of everything that was right. He had a wonderful time, along with the other grandchildren, at the big party at Grandfather Ezekiel's when the Polks and their neighbors gathered to celebrate Jefferson's election.

When he was a little older, Jimmy was sent to the log cabin school not far from his home. He walked the short distance and neighbors who saw him plodding along the rutted clay road later recalled that he was a mighty shy little boy. He learned the basic lessons of reading and writing, but his schooling wasn't regular. With his health none too good, he was kept home in bad weather. The school itself was closed now and then for lack of a teacher. Such routine lessons as he received gave him none of the inspiration for study that came later.

Meanwhile, Grandfather Ezekiel had begun to tire of the crusade for religious freedom that had kept the county so upset and had started to talk again of the rich lands across the mountains in Tennessee. With Jefferson as President, he foresaw a time of booming opportunity and tried to arouse the rest of the Polks to join him in the adventure that awaited on the new frontier. Jimmy's father couldn't be convinced. He was doing well where he was, had added to his lands and was prospering, and

Ezekiel's talk of the new country seemed to promise less than what he already had. Besides, Jimmy's mother had flatly refused to leave her own family and friends, her comfortable home and settled life, for the hardships there would be in starting all over again in Tennessee.

But Ezekiel did manage to persuade his married daughter and three of his other sons to leave Mecklenburg and go with him. He promised them all farms next to his own plantation and in 1803 he gathered together the eager members of the clan, with all their children, and led them off in a caravan which left Sam and his family behind. From their new plantations in the Red River country of Middle Tennessee, Ezekiel soon sent back glowing reports of the tobacco and cotton crops, of the prosperity he still urged Sam to share. Sam answered that he was content in Mecklenburg.

It took three years of urging and the opening up of Indian territory in Tennessee to change his mind. Ezekiel had moved again, into what was to become Maury County, to lands he had set his heart on during his first surveying trip into Tennessee. Taking children and grandchildren with him, he had settled at last in a fertile valley north of Duck River, and he begged Sam to come west.

Many of Sam's neighbors in Mecklenburg were pulling up stakes and heading for Tennessee. Everywhere, there was talk of migrating, and the movement grew until trains of wagons filled the roads. Jimmy had brothers and sisters by then and Sam began to think of the future, of the opportunity his sons might have in a place where there was more room for growth than in North Carolina. Ezekiel promised him plenty of work as a surveyor while he was getting his first crops planted. Jimmy's mother was still reluctant to leave, but she finally agreed she shouldn't stand in the way of the better chance there might be for her boys in Tennessee.

Sam finally made up his mind that summer of 1806. When the crops were in, the family planned to go. Tennessee was so far away, it seemed to Jimmy like getting ready to journey into another world. For days before they left, friends and relatives came to say their farewells, knowing that they might never see each other again. He was excited over the great adventure that lay ahead as he packed the few boyhood treasures he would be allowed to take in the crowded wagon. Among the grown-ups, there were tearful partings, but he was only eager to be on the way.

Early in the morning, with the last of the belongings put aboard, the wagon started up the road through Charlotte and then to the north and west. Jimmy walked beside his father and his two sisters, eight-year-old Eliza and six-year-old Jane, although they were allowed in the wagon when they were tired. His brother, Franklin, who was only four, and his other brother, Marshall, still a baby, had to ride with their mother. Now and then, Jimmy rode for a short spell on one of the horses, but most of his travel was on foot. Over the smoother stretches of road, they could cover nearly twenty miles a day.

For the most part, the going was much slower. Fall rains had turned the rutted roads to sticky mud and there was more pulling and hauling than easy travel. When the wagon became stuck, Jimmy and all the others helped by putting their shoulders to it while the horses strained to pull it free. But the Polks weren't alone. There were other wagons and they joined in companies so that all hands could help. There were streams to ford and still the danger of Indians in some places. At night, when they camped and Jimmy joined the boys from the other wagons, he heard frightening stories told around the campfires about bandits who had attacked some of the wagon trains.

The mountains loomed ahead of them, seeming to rise higher as they came close, until a steep wall of rock shut off the narrow valley. There was no way except to haul the wagons straight up, one at a time, by ropes. Jimmy joined the men in that, although he was soon exhausted and had to rest. Beyond, there was a rough stretch of flat land for a few days, and then more mountains, steeper than before. But as they descended at last into the valleys of Eastern Tennessee, there were signs of settlement, cabins and cleared fields. At last, they reached Knoxville, and briefly enjoyed the comforts of civilization. Jimmy said goodbye there to some of the wagon trail friends he had made.

For him and his family, there were still miles to go, across the Cumberland plateau. They had to stock up on food enough to last them and they were warned again of the outlaw gangs that roamed the wilderness ahead. But after another week of travel, they took the long road down, turned south, and within three days were at Grandfather Ezekiel's place. There was a joyful reunion then for Jimmy with all his cousins.

Everybody remarked about how much he had grown since they had seen him last, and talk of the trip went on into the night. But as happy as he was to be there, Jimmy was even happier to tumble into a soft bed. They had been on the road for a month and a half and nobody could blame an eleven-year-old boy for being tired after walking most of five hundred miles.

Chapter Two

THE TOWERING TREES of the deep forest made Jim Polk feel even smaller than he was as he rode with his father through the wild and lonely country Grandfather Ezekiel had called a promised land. When they turned from the dirt trail, the way was choked with thick cane that grew half as high as the trees and nearly walled out the sun. This was to be his home, here in the wildernes where there was nothing, where his own hands would have to help in making good whatever the rough earth promised. He looked around him and was homesick for everything that had been sure about his life in North Carolina.

But he helped his father and the other men cut the cane and drag it into piles for burning, ducking back as the dry stalks exploded like pistol shots in the roaring flames. With his ax, he trimmed the small branches from the giant logs that were hewn to build the cabin. All the neighbors came for the house raising, to set the logs into place and to turn the work into fun, and at last there was a home. He felt better about it then. But his own days began at dawn and ended when it was too dark to see, with little time for play.

With the cabin up and more of the fields cleared, there was tobacco to be planted to bring in money, corn needed for food, and flax for the clothing his mother would make. Around the house and in the fields, there were endless chores for Jim to do. That first winter he had a warm suit of dressed buckskin to wear, soft and velvety when it was new, but soon stiff and hard and so icy cold to put on some mornings that he could hardly keep his teeth from chattering.

The farm prospered and other settlers built cabins in the valleys and along the jagged streams that flowed into the Duck River. His father led the neighbors in petitioning the legislature to create the new county of Maury. He soon became one of the the chosen leaders who helped to plan the town of Columbia that was to be the new county seat. Jim watched the laying out of the town, only six miles down the road from his home, saw the first log courthouse built there, facing a muddy clearing that was set aside as a public square. When his father became a county magistrate, Jim was sometimes allowed to go with him into the booming little town, to sit at the back of the courtroom.

Sundays, after worship, families gathered at one cabin or another to enjoy their one day of relaxation with less strictness than there had been in keeping the Sabbath back in Mecklenburg. Jim joined the other boys, shooting marbles, playing ball, going off for the afternoon to fish in the creek. There were wild grapes to pick and nuts to gather, slingshots to try and bows and arrows to shoot. His mother cautioned him when he became too loud, reminded him that the day was the Lord's, but she knew it was the only time he had to himself and she hadn't the heart to be too stern with him.

There were times when he had to drop out of the

games, his energy quickly spent, and some Sundays when he was too exhausted from the week's work to play. His father worried because he wasn't as strong as the other boys, couldn't compete with them, although it was never for lack of courage. Jim got into wrestling matches in which he knew he would be beaten and foot races he was bound to lose. Sometimes when he tried to jump over a low tree limb or swing by his hands from branch to branch, so bad a pain would seize his stomach he had to fight to keep from crying out.

Sam Polk hated to see his son a loser. What Jim needed, he decided, was toughening up. He took him with him on surveying trips that led them through the forests and canebrakes for weeks at a time, camping in the woods, measuring off the vast distances step by step with rods and chains, until Jim could hardly drag his feet. His legs and back ached, but he tried to hide it from his father because he didn't want to be thought a weakling. He drove himself to make up with determination for his lack of strength.

His father realized that instead of building his health, the outdoor life and exercise seemed to wear Jim down. As the surveying business grew, Sam took other men along to do the harder tasks and put Jim to keeping camp, cooking the meals, tending the horses. Jim enjoyed it when his father let him help with the mapping and the figuring. Although he had been given little schooling before he left North Carolina and less since, he was quick at adding the numbers called out to him and in solving simple problems of mathematics.

Surveying had been a way for Sam to bring the family extra money, but it became more important to him than the farm. New settlers frequently paid him for his surveying with part of the land. Knowing the country so well, Sam was able to buy other lands and to sell his holdings at a high profit. Through the Polks in North Carolina, he acted as agent for thousands of acres of valuable Tennessee property. Land sales became his main interest and as his fortunes increased Sam spent more time in town and less on surveying trips with Jim.

As Jim came into his teens, he saw the trail in front of the house become a main road leading into Columbia while the town itself was the center of a peaceful and settled farming community. But to his family, it seemed that he had turned his back on all of it. When he wasn't sick, he found other reasons for avoiding effort, idled away his hours without any real ambition or interest in anything, unless it was to ride over to Grandfather Ezekiel's now and then to borrow a book and lose himself in reading. When his mother scolded or his father grew angry, he would do what he was told, but with no spirit and no liking for what he had to do.

The fateful year of 1812, which brought the still young United States to war, disrupted the calm of Maury County in so many ways Jim's parents probably didn't realize at first that he was facing a serious crisis of his own. The county's troubles really began late the year before, just about the time Jim was turning sixteen. The Duck River went on a rampage that sent destructive floods sweeping into the lowlands, and people had hardly recovered before the area was struck by a series of earthquakes that came every few days over a period of nearly three months. They weren't severe, but before they ended in the spring of 1812 bewildered settlers were so frightened some of them were convinced the land was cursed and talked of abandoning their homes.

Still more trouble came when the Indians, who had been peaceful for many years, staged an uprising and a family was massacred by a marauding party of Creeks. Men took down their guns and began oiling them. In Columbia, military drills were held to practice bush fighting and defense against tomahawking. The militia turned out in force, but almost before they could get into action the news came that the long-festering conflict with Britain had put the whole nation at war. People in the west, anxious to expand their lands, suspected the British of arming the Indians and backing them in their uprisings, so the Indians as well as the British became the enemy. When Andrew Jackson, as Major General of the Tennessee militia, called for troops to accompany him on an expedition to occupy West Florida, Maury County supplied 2,500 volunteers.

With so much happening to disturb the county, Sam and Jane Polk were too upset to pay much attention to Jim's personal problems. As sickly as he had been most of his life and as moody as he had been lately, they still hoped he would outgrow whatever was ailing him. Doctors were not called every time a boy "acted poorly," especially not on the frontier. Medical attention, even when it could be had, was none too good. But finally they were shocked into realizing something was desperately wrong when Jim doubled over with shooting spasms of pain that stabbed from his stomach to his back and right shoulder in a repeated agony which filled his eyes with tears he couldn't conceal.

Sam got him to a doctor then, as soon as he could. But the examination wasn't swift or easy and when it was made there seemed little that could be done. The diagnosis was gallstone and an operation might be possible, but not in Tennessee, nor anywhere with more than a slim hope that Jim would live through it. Abdominal surgery was a seldom-practiced risk, so unusual that every successful operation was heralded in the newspapers as an achievement of medical science. Disheartened, his father took Jim home, understanding at last that much of his recent tiredness and the lack of ambition for which they had blamed him was due to his condition.

The Polks had many friends and Sam sought the advice of those who might know more about the new surgery than he could learn from local doctors. Some warned him that a sick boy was better than a dead one and that it was best to let Jim live out his remaining years as an invalid, protected as much as possible from any activity that might cause him pain. But from a newspaper clipping that was sent to him, Jim's father learned about Doctor Ephriam Mc Dowell.

Mc Dowell, who had studied at the University of Edinburgh and had taken personal instruction from the celebrated Scotch anatomist, John Bell, had settled in Danville, Kentucky, where he had won a reputation as the best surgeon west of Philadelphia. The newspaper article told of his daring first successful abdominal operations, which later were to gain him recognition as one of the founders of that type of surgery in America. With ideas boldly contrary to some of the best-accepted medical practices of the time, he was to perform more than thirty gallstone operations. But when Sam Polk read of him, Mc Dowell's fame was only beginning, and it took faith and courage to decide he would put his son's life in the doctor's hands.

Jim's mother needed courage, too, as she sent him and his father on their way after the arrangements had been made. For Jim, the ordeal must have been a terrifying one, knowing that he faced an experience few people had gone through. The trip itself was not easy. On horseback, at his father's side, he suffered days of rough and painful travel that led them more than two hundred miles to Danville and the simple white frame house that was Mc Dowell's home as well as his office and hospital.

Jim was so weakened by the trip and by his illness that the first thing Mc Dowell did was to order him to bed for several weeks of complete rest and care before he would attempt the operation. In those weeks, Jim got to know the doctor well, to like him and to trust him. Mc Dowell wasn't the coldly serious man of medical science Jim had expected him to be. He was big and hearty, a strong-bodied man, vigorous and athletic by nature, given to deep laughter and a quick sense of humor, warmly friendly and considerate.

In later years, Mc Dowell frankly admitted that he hadn't seen much promise in Jim Polk. He remembered the boy as a "thin, emaciated stripling," poorly educated and physically weak, not the sort of a lad he then guessed would get far in the world. But he also remembered Jim's bravery, the inner toughness that had surprised him in a boy who looked so weak.

Even under Mc Dowell's skilled hands, the operation took all the courage Jim could muster. He was given a glass of brandy to help dull his senses a little, but there were no anesthetics to deaden the real agony of pain or to put him mercifully to sleep until it was over. Fully conscious of what was being done to him, Jim was strapped to a plain wooden table and held down by two male assistants while Mc Dowell made the incision. There was grave danger of infection because true antiseptics were unknown. But Mc Dowell removed the stone, later gave it to Jim as a souvenir, and the operation was successful despite all the odds against it. After a few weeks more in Danville to regain his strength, Jim and his father started the long ride home to Tennessee.

By the time they reached Columbia, Jim already seemed a different boy. Partly it was because of his returning health, but perhaps because he had faced death, or at least the knowledge that he might die, and had won over it and was jubilantly alive. He had also faced himself and discovered a firmness of character and courage he would never again have to doubt. He might not be tall or big and powerful, not strong in body even after the operation, but there were other ways in which he could make himself a match for any man. Jim had found what he never had before, belief in himself as a person.

For a while, he was a celebrity in Maury County, among his friends and all the Polks who wanted to hear about his experience and to see the stone that had been taken out of him. The newly-started newspaper in Columbia published an account of the event. But long before the excitement died down, Jim had become tired of telling about his operation. He had a new ambition that, for a boy who had been accused of having none, was suddenly intense. He had a passionate desire to make up for the schooling he had lost. The books he had borrowed now and then from Grandfather Ezekiel, in the dull days when nothing but reading had interested him, now became a doorway to that ambition.

He had a thirst for all the learning that had been denied him on the frontier because he realized that only by learning could he make himself the equal of other men. Mc Dowell had been an example to him and he thought maybe he would become a doctor, or perhaps a minister, which would greatly please his mother. Then again, he might be a lawyer or a judge, might even be a leader in politics because the Polks had always been good at that. Jim wasn't sure what he wanted to be, only sure that his future lay in one of the professions rather than in the work of his hands and that education was the way to achieve it.

Grandfather Ezekiel's library was only a start. Jim soon was borrowing books from any neighbor who happened to have a volume or two and would lend them. But when he spoke to his father about wanting to go to school somewhere to prepare himself for college, Sam Polk was reluctant to make any promises. College was for the very few and Jim had never shown himself to be brilliant or much of a scholar. His father told him he had better give up such ideas and learn a trade that would earn him a solid living.

If Jim was disappointed, he also was more determined than ever to impress his father. He laid out a plan of study for himself from the books available to him, spent every waking hour learning from them. He tried to enlist his mother's sympathy and even tried to get Grandfather Ezekiel to put in a word for him with his father. But Sam Polk became concerned that Jim was wearing himself out, shutting himself off from other people, and that something definite had to be done.

He talked to Jim about a future in the business world, with the state growing in population and commerce prospering—the real success he saw in that for a young man willing to start at the bottom and learn merchandising. Jim was quick with figures, had a level head, would be in an occupation that didn't tax his physical strength, and many opportunities might present themselves once he had his feet on the ground. When Jim protested that it wasn't what he wanted to do, his father silenced him and said he had made up his mind it would be the best thing for him.

Acting on his decision, Sam rode into Columbia and made arrangements with the owner of the general store to take Jim on as a helper and teach him the business in exchange for his work. Because of the Polks' influence in the community, the storekeeper was willing. He told Jim what had been arranged and said that someday Jim would thank him for giving him a good start in life.

Jim begged and pleaded, then finally had to give in. But with his mind set on being a doctor or lawyer, somebody who would be looked up to as a person of importance, he was completely miserable behind the store counter. Selling loaves of sugar, weighing out bags of salt, and measuring off lengths of calico for the farm wives seemed a wearisome task after the excitement of the world of ideas he had found in books. Unable to keep his mind on the work, he made mistakes, mixed up orders, and was so unhappily out of place that the merchant finally told his father Jim wasn't cut out to be a storekeeper.

Seeing how really unhappy Jim was, his father agreed to let him leave the store and said that maybe a year or two of schooling might be best for him after all. But he made no promise of college and Jim knew it was up to him to win that chance by proving his ability. His ambition took a definite direction that April of 1813 when Andrew Jackson came to Columbia after marching his volunteers back up the long trail from the lower Mississippi. The Jacksons and Polks had been close since the settlement days in the Carolinas when the families first met and the General had become even better acquainted with Sam Polk in Tennessee. During his visit to Columbia, Jackson was Sam's guest for dinner. Jim was in the cheering crowd that welcomed him and later was able to sit close to him at the table when Jackson was entertained in his own home.

If Jefferson had been Jim's first hero as a boy, Jackson

became his hero then. The General was still to win the national fame that would come after his campaign against the Creeks and his spectacular victory over the British invaders at New Orleans at the end of the war. Still, he was already an important figure in the country's political and military life and had a firm place in the hearts of the people of Tennessee. He had helped to draft the state's constitution, had served Tennessee in Congress and had been a judge of the Superior Court before taking command of the militia. Jackson's career and his popularity greatly impressed Jim. This was the sort of man he wanted to be, not a doctor or a minister, but a leader of the people, one who helped shape their politics and their government.

Three months later, Jim entered the little academy that the Presbyterian congregation had set up in Zion Church several miles south of Columbia. Thus, in his eighteenth year, his first real education began. Mostly self-taught until then, rich in the learning he had found in books, he lacked the formal training that had put his classmates well ahead of him. Jim could write, but his penmanship was crude. He could read, but his spelling was poor. With hardly any preparation, he was expected to study the Latin classics, part of the Greek testament, and all the other subjects in the usual academic course of the time.

Instead of discouraging him, the challenge was a tonic to him, everything he had been thirsting for, and he worked at his lessons as though he had to squeeze out every drop of learning to be had from them. Older than the other boys, he felt he had to study harder than they did, to make up for every hour of education he had lost. The school was taught by a highly educated and greatly respected Presbyterian minister, the Reverend Robert

Henderson. He was a strict man who disciplined unruly boys by turning them over to an elder of the church who took them down to the spring for a stern lecture and a sound birching when necessary, but he had no trouble with Jim, who was too glad of the opportunity to be in school to misbehave.

Henderson soon discovered he had a prize pupil in Jim and encouraged him in every way possible. Perhaps Jim surprised even himself when he went to the head of the class. He certainly impressed his father, who was amazed to discover his son possessed such hidden ability. From Henderson's example, Jim also learned his first lessons in public speaking. For all his stern manner, Henderson had a lively sense of humor, a sharp wit and talent for mimicry that he used to advantage when he spoke to the boys. He could act out a funny story in a way that drove home the point he was making better than any lecture, a technique Jim later was to use so tellingly in his own political debates.

When the year ended, Sam Polk was so pleased by his son's progress that it was he who suggested sending him to a better school. It was one of the state's leading academies, conducted by Samuel Black, who had a reputation as an outstanding educator. Black's school, the Bradley Academy, was in Murfreesboro, some fifty miles from Columbia. Sam arranged for Jim to board there with a family who lived near the large log building where classes were held.

On his own in town surroundings that were quite different from the frontier home in which he had grown up, and far more confident of himself, Jim began to lose his rustic awkwardness and became an attractive young man. Although still below average height, he was fair-haired, clear-eyed, and had rather handsome features, along with a neat appearance and a manner that began to attract the attention of some of the town's young girls. Jim enjoyed their company and frequently was invited to dine by the townspeople and the parents of his classmates. But his studies took most of his time. In addition to Greek and Latin, his subjects included mathematics, geography, philosophy, ethics, history of religion, astronomy, literature and logic.

One of his friends at school was Anderson Childress, the son of a leading businessman who lived a few miles outside Murfreesboro. In the afternoons, after regular classes for the boys of the school had been finished, Anderson's two little sisters, Sarah and Susan, were brought to the academy for private lessons since there was no good school for girls in the area. Their father, Joel Childress, was a fairly wealthy man and Jim was probably impressed by their beautiful clothes and how pretty they looked. But since Sarah was only eleven at the time, it isn't likely he really paid much attention to her. Certainly he couldn't have guessed he someday would fall in love with her and make her his wife.

By the time the academy's year-end exercises were held in 1815, Jim topped his classmates in scholastic achievement. He also had a lead part in a class play, in which he proved himself a fair comedian by portraying the role of "Jerry Sneak." When he delivered the class oration, making good use of the mimicry he had learned from Parson Henderson, a newspaper account of the affair described him as showing "the finest capacity for public speaking ever heard in a youth." With all his talents, Jim stood out as "much the most promising young man in the school."

It didn't take much urging from Samuel Black to convince Jim's father he should send the boy on to college.

On his own and with everything against him, Jim had won the chance to make good his ambition. He was so happy he could hardly talk of anything else during the trip back to Columbia with his father.

There wasn't much question as to which college he would attend. The University of North Carolina already was becoming one of the leading educational institutions of the south and Sam's cousin, William Polk, was among its most active trustees. Sam himself had been real estate agent for some of the Tennessee lands owned by the college and the state was Jim's birthplace. With all the ties he already had there, that much was quickly decided.

It was only after the letter had been written to seek his admission that Jim began to worry. Hard work had gotten him through Parson Henderson's school and through the academy, but he still had little schooling. He had confidence in himself, but not the confidence a whole life of schooling would have given him. Despite his father's willingness to send him, he knew that if he failed, there would be no second chance. He had to make good, or lose everything in life he wanted.

Chapter Three

VISITING RELATIVES and family friends along the way, Jim Polk traveled the five hundred miles into North Carolina over the lands he had come across as a boy when his folks first pioneered into Tennessee. In spirit, there was still much of the frontier in the busy new communities and flourishing farms that surrounded them, but the area seemed to be turning to a new way of life, just as he was.

He spent a little time in Mecklenburg, revisiting the places of his childhood and enjoying reunions with the Polks who had remained there, but he was too eager to get on to Chapel Hill to stay long. Yet as he turned his horse up the last road to the high ridge upon which the few buildings of the university were clustered, his mind filled with anxiety. He was determined not to allow himself any doubt. They must accept him. But he wanted it so much, he felt sweat break out on his forehead and wet his shirt across his shoulders, even though the day was cool.

His interview with the university's president, the Reverend Robert Chapman, went well. He was able to satisfy him as to his general intelligence and good moral character. His Presbyterian upbringing helped when it came to answering the questions of religious faith Chapman asked, since all instruction at the university was carried on strictly according to those beliefs. Being an ardent young Jeffersonian, Jim probably kept his political opinions to himself, knowing Chapman had strong Federalist views.

Chapman made appointments for him to visit each of the instructors. There were no written examinations, but he was searchingly questioned by each man to determine his ability to meet the basic requirements of English grammar, the Latin of Caesar's Commentaries, Virgil's poetry, Sallust's history, and the Greek of the Gospel of St. John. To his great relief, the examiners finally agreed that he seemed qualified to enter the sophomore class at the start of the second term in January, 1816.

It was only then that Jim began to take a real look around. He and the university were the same age, both starting their twenty-first year. The faculty was still small. In addition to Chapman and several instructors and tutors, including two graduate students who taught the lower classes, the only full professor was Doctor Joseph Caldwell, in charge of mathematics. Caldwell soon would replace Chapman as president and add to the university's staff as well as broaden its outlook.

Jim paid his tuition of ten dollars for the term and his room rent of a dollar and strolled beneath the tall oaks and hickories across the broad park of uncut grass and underbrush that was the center of the campus. Called "Grand Avenue," it led toward the village of Chapel Hill, a place of two stores, a tavern and a dozen homes. Fronting the park was Old East, the original university building, by then a dormitory. A plain structure, two stories high, it had been built of bricks made of clay from the university's lands and with sea shells that were converted to lime.

The South Building, where he would have his classes, included a library and rooms for the university's debating societies as well as more dormitories on its three floors. Earlier students had built their own living huts there, but a lottery two years before had raised enough money to complete the building. On opposite sides of the park there were a simple chapel and a large frame house known as Steward's Hall, where Jim learned he could get a year's meals for forty dollars, unless he decided to make other eating arrangements. Some of the college men ate in the village or cooked their own food and a few brought servants with them to forage for firewood and prepare their meals. In the dormitories, there were plain wooden bunks and poorer students slept on the hard boards, with perhaps a blanket or some straw for a bed. But Jim discovered that for twelve dollars a term he could rent a feather bed from the steward.

He was awakened at six in the morning by the ringing bell in the cupola of the New College building on his first day of classes and had fifteen minutes to dress and get to chapel for morning prayers. After breakfast, the sophomore class instructor, William Hooper, outlined the course Jim would study during the term. It was to include a solid grounding in Greek and Roman literature and constant drilling in English grammar as well as some geography and Biblical and classical history. From early morning until late afternoon, his time would be spent at lectures and in recitations, with a brief period for fun and relaxation until evening prayer at five. After supper, he would be on his own until the study bell rang, at eight in the winter months and nine during the summer, to send the men to their rooms for study until bedtime.

Sundays were to be devoted to strict observance of the Sabbath, with all the students expected to don black gowns to attend public worship at the chapel. He would have to give some of the day to Bible study, since the instructors would examine him from time to time and failure to satisfy them as to his religious views or high moral conduct could bring immediate dismissal from the university. Both president Chapman and Professor Caldwell, whose classes Jim didn't enter until his junior year, were ministers who looked to the Presbyterians' College of New Jersey, later to be known as Princeton University, as the model for their own efforts in North Carolina.

Jim attacked his studies with the same determination he had shown at school in Tennessee. He set a record at the university by never missing a recitation or chapel exercise and never being late for a class. It wasn't long before his reputation for promptness became a campus legend. His admiring instructors joked that they could set their clocks by his comings and goings and one of them commented that nothing in the world was more certain than "that Jim Polk will be up tomorrow morning at the ringing of the first bell."

But for all his devotion to learning, he enjoyed campus life and was popular with his classmates. Most of them were as serious about their studies as he was and they approved his ambition and began to seek his friendship. He had never really had close friends before, since his childhood had been clouded by the feeling that he would be inadequate to the rough and tumble activities by which a frontier boy was judged. But at the university, men became leaders by a different standard and he was able to match his mind against any. His personality grew warmer, more friendly and less reserved, as he found himself accepted and welcomed. He soon was making the sort of friendships that lasted all his life.

Among his friends was William Green, later a minister, professor at the university and then first Episcopal bishop of Mississippi, and one of the founders of the University of the South at Sewanee, Tennessee. Another of his companions, although they often had hot arguments over politics, was high-spirited Hugh Waddell, frequently the ringleader in college extra-curricular activities. Waddell went on to study medicine, abandoned that to become a lawyer, and finally was a North Carolina senator. Ham Jones, also a fun-maker, was to be a newspaper editor, and Will Haywood, who shared some of Jim's adventures, would serve in the United States Senate when Jim became President.

Campus life centered around the two literary societies, each of which had its own hall in New College, and Jim was invited to join the Dialectic Society at the start of his first term. Its keen rival was the Philanthropic Society. The debates and essay contests held by the "Di" and the "Phi" were as important in those days as football games of much later years. Most of the students sided with one group or the other and each ruled its own clique, so that being chosen a leader of one of the societies was a guarantee of campus popularity.

The talent Jim had shown for public speaking grew rapidly in the Dialectic Society's weekly debates and the meetings became his chief interest, aside from his studies. He spent hours working on the topics to be debated, lining up his arguments and digging into books for the facts to support them. His wit and ability to drive home a point with comic satire won him new respect as one of the university's outstanding speakers. In the essay competitions, he was a constant winner, and eight of his papers took special honors.

He was elected the society's treasurer and then its secretary. As such, he had a voice in nearly all campus activities. Although he was a loyal "Di," he also made good friends among the "Phis." One of his chief opponents in the Philanthropic Society was his pal John Mason, an upperclassman from Virginia who went on to a career in Congress and as a Federal judge before becoming Secretary of the Navy under President Tyler and then a member of Polk's own cabinet after he was President.

As the weather grew warmer and they had more time for fun before the evening study bell, Jim often went into the village with Will Haywood and his other friends, to visit the stores and strike up an acquaintance with the girls in town. They sometimes had supper at a house run by a Mrs. Puckett, who served puddings made from soaked biscuits that were considered a special treat. But an even more lively attraction was a village belle whom Jim was not alone in admiring. Although his romantic interest probably never went beyond trying to coax a smile or two from her, his friends later recalled that the girl, fondly called "Betts Puss," seemed to think Jim was quite a dashing young man.

Other evenings he spent walking through the nearby woods with friends, carrying on impromptu debates, or else he did some extra study in his room. He was called upon several times to deliver orations to the school after evening prayer and his leadership of various committees of the "Di" also kept him busy. The books he contributed to the society's library included a set of the *Decline and Fall of the Roman Empire* and a biography of Andrew Jackson. Among the volumes Jim borrowed for his own outside reading were studies of the Constitution and a history of the Revolution.

When the term ended in June and a committee of university trustees arrived to give the students the usual public examinations, James Polk took first rank in his class. He had a six-week recess then, before he started his first term as a junior. Worn out by his hard study and all his other activities, he spent the time with Carolina relatives, relaxing and hardly looking at a book. When he returned to the university in July, his roommate was William Moseley, who was to become the closest of all his friends at college and later first governor of Florida.

Jim also came under the direct influence, for the first time, of the real intellectual leader of the university, Doctor Caldwell, who taught him not only mathematics but also a love for logic and simplicity in words and thoughts. From the time of his boyhood surveying trips with his father, Jim had realized he was good at figures, but it was Caldwell who helped him develop the strongly logical nature of his own mind until he had a "passionate fondness" for mathematics. Caldwell, a graduate of the College of New Jersey, had written his own text for his geometry class and started Jim and the others off by having them make manuscript copies of it. The hand-copying was tedious work, but it gave them a broad view of the entire subject before detailed study began. Caldwell was no man to tolerate fuzzy thinking or let any student get by with less than an absolute understanding of each problem and he challenged Jim to his best efforts.

The result was a deepening of all his thought. His essays for the Dialectic Society ranged from a patriotic defense of every man's right to an equal voice in government to a paper on the powers of invention, Locke's psychology and Newton's genius. In debates, he argued the question of extending American territory, won a contest on the issue that there was no conflict between the practice of law and "the pure precepts of Christianity," and defeated another opponent by proving that the life of a statesman was preferable to that of a warrior. On a less serious topic, Jim convinced his listeners that "an occasional resort to female company" was beneficial to students.

Sometimes the debates grew so excited he and another member were fined ten cents for hurling threats at each other that nearly led to a fight with fists instead of words. He paid several other fines for breaking the society's stiff rules, for being absent from meetings on evenings he and Moseley chose to go into town, and once was charged with "gross irregularity" for a joke he played.

But there was little enough fun to relieve the heavy pressure of his studies. Night after night, as Moseley recalled, they kept the candle burning late in their room where they "spent so many tedious and laborious hours attempting to discover the beauties of Cicero and Homer and in less interesting amusements of quadratic equations and composition." By the end of the term, Jim and his roommate, Moseley, shared honors as the best scholars in their class.

He and Moseley spent the month of winter vacation together in Raleigh, visiting a wealthy cousin of Jim's, enjoying parties, dances and a round of social activities. Jim seemed especially attracted for a while to one of the young ladies he met, but his interest in his career was stronger than in romance and he was anxious to get back to the university when vacation was over. On his return to the campus, the Dialectic Society elected him president. In a ringing address, he told its members that reason could reach its highest potential only under a free government "where genius in rags can aspire to promotion."

But it was in the give and take of debate, rather than in his set speeches, that he learned the techniques which were to serve him so well during his political stumping tours of Tennessee and when he later led the debates in Congress. As a practical school of statesmanship, his presidency of the "Di" probably taught him more than his studies in the university's classrooms. Settling disputes and rivalries, bringing various factions together, weighing his own friendships and popularity against the decisions he was required to make, he did so well that the society broke its established rule and re-elected him president again in his senior year.

Looking ahead to the career in politics that was his own ambition, Jim realized that many of his fellow members of the "Di" might reach high position. "You may be called upon to succeed those who now stand as the representatives of the people, to wield by the thunder of your eloquence the council of a great nation and to retain by your prudent measures that liberty for which our fathers bled," he told them in his address, accepting the society's presidency. Whatever their future might be, he added, "your proficiency in extemporaneous debating will furnish you with that fluency of language, the connection of ideas and boldness of delivery, that will be equally serviceable in the council, at the pulpit and at the bar."

He was right in guessing that there were many among his classmates who would become eminent as Senators, Congressmen, cabinet members, diplomats and college presidents as well as lawyers, clergymen, and businessmen. But few could have guessed he someday would be the most famous of all, even though there was a maturity in his thinking, a logic and directness, an enormous growth in discovering how to make the most of himself, which had come of his college years.

In the classrooms, Caldwell once again was his inspiration, as Jim's teacher in philosophy now. From his own student days at the College of New Jersey, Caldwell had kept his notes of the lectures delivered by the great John Witherspoon. These were what opened Jim's mind to deep and enlightening questions about ethics, religion, and man's existence. Under Elisha Mitchell, a new professor Caldwell had brought from Yale, Jim's senior class was the first to have the benefit of what was advanced teaching of science for those days.

In his own debates and speeches, Jim showed his determination to strip away the flowery language of his earlier years. He began to develop a simplicity of style that was to mark his later addresses and public papers. Speaking to the members of the "Di" about true eloquence, he said there was "often too much attention paid to the elegance of language and too little to the ideas conveyed by it" and that the "studied metaphors and flowers of language" were no substitute for a fluent and bold delivery in words that came naturally from a mind "entirely engrossed by the subject which it is considering."

As his final term drew to an end, he gave less time to campus activities and pleasant excursions into town with his friends. He seemed to feel the hours were running out before he had a chance to get the most from them and almost to regret every minute he had spent on fun as a waste of time. He worried that he hadn't learned enough and although he had never neglected his studies, he drove himself to them with a new frenzy of effort. He went without meals sometimes and often without sleep. His health suffered and there were days when he felt really sick, but he would allow himself no excuses. He shut himself in his room with his books and shunned everything that might tempt him from them.

When the university's twelve trustees arrived at Chapel Hill the end of May, 1818, Jim faced the full week of examinations as though they were a personal challenge to prove himself against every student on the campus. If there were others who were more brilliant certainly none were better prepared. He was judged top scholar in his class and the best in the entire university in his knowledge of the classics and in mathematics. It was a proud victory for Jim, one of the proudest of his life, a measure of his growth from the awkward Tennessee frontier boy who, until five years before, had hardly been inside a classroom.

Graduation filled Chapel Hill with parents and relatives, alumni who had become leading figures in political and business life, a crowd of visitors who filled all available rooms in the village and surrounding farmhouses. The commencement ball was the social event of the year for Jim and the other seniors. Dressed in a green coat with a high velvet collar and silver buttons, a cambric stock around his neck and a cravat and ruffled shirt, he wore a white damask vest, pantaloons and flesh-colored stockings, low-cut and silver-buckled pumps. His dancing partners, the sisters and cousins of his friends, attired in their formal ball gowns of silk and satin, helped make it an evening to remember, and nobody enjoyed it more than Jim.

But it represented a parting from the college that had given him so much, from the campus where he had become a chosen leader, leaving friends who had been closer to him than his own brothers. It was the custom for best friends to exchange mementoes and Jim presented Will Moseley with an ornamental pin he would keep all his life as a token of the days he had shared as Jim's roommate at Chapel Hill.

In the chapel on the last day, as the school's leading scholar, Jim delivered the salutatory address in Latin.

But when the ceremonies were over, when the goodbyes had been said and the crowd had departed, he was too exhausted to start his own journey home. The overwork and self-imposed ordeal of final study had brought him close to a complete breakdown.

He stayed with relatives in North Carolina, was invited to the home of friends near the university and now and then visited the campus again for a day to borrow books from the library. His father came to see him late in July, but Jim's condition was still too poor for the long trip to Tennessee. Resting in the country, slowly getting back on his feet, he had long hours to himself to plan the future, days of riding his horse along the peaceful wooded trails and restoring his health in the outdoors.

He at last started home in early October. His energy had returned and ambition hurried him once more. Time enough had been lost now that Jim Polk had decided on the next goal he would fight to achieve.

Chapter Four

THE HOME James Polk returned to in the fall of 1818 was far different from the one he had left. Business was booming and his father had moved the family from the farm into one of the best houses in Columbia. It was white brick and two stories high, with French windows that opened out from spacious rooms upon a balcony that overlooked the bustling community where cotton had become king.

His sister Jane was now the wife of James Walker, owner of the town's newspaper and his father's partner in a dozen profitable enterprises. Together, Sam Polk and Walker owned Columbia's biggest store, took in cotton and tobacco from all the surrounding plantations for shipment to New Orleans, had a contract to furnish provisions to the Indians and another with the Post Office Department to carry mail from Nashville to the southwest. Walker was president of the new bank and Sam a director. They were organizing a company to build a road from Columbia to the Tennessee River, another to operate steamboats, and Sam was buying and selling thousands of acres of land.

Settlers were streaming into the state as never before,

new buildings were going up everywhere, money was easy and bank notes were pouring into the economy as fast as the banks could print them. Cotton was bringing high prices and everything else was riding on the crest of inflation. Everybody James met on the street proudly boasted how Columbia was growing. His own family had grown, too. Another sister, Lydia, had married the town's leading doctor. But there were two more sisters and five brothers still at home. Naomi was ten and Ophelia was six. He hardly recognized Franklin, who had been just a youngster and was now sixteen. Marshall and John were much taller than they had been and three-year-old William was toddling around on his own. The youngest of all, baby Samuel, was carried out to greet him in his mother's arms.

It was a noisy, happy home, and there was so much news to tell at the big dinner table that James had to wait until after the children's bedtime to discuss his own plans with his father. He told him his mind was set on a political career but that he first wanted to become a lawyer. It would mean more study and hard work as a clerk in some established lawyer's office until he had learned enough to take the bar examination, but it would give him a profession as well as a chance to feel his way in politics.

Sam said that his decision was a wise one and suggested that the man to teach him was Felix Grundy of Nashville. Grundy was a national political figure as well as an outstanding orator and a clever courtroom lawyer. In Congress, he had been one of the War Hawks who supported the War of 1812, which the Federalists blamed on "Madison, Grundy and the Devil." He was at the center of Tennessee politics and had established a reputation as the best criminal attorney in the west. It was said that Grundy's courtroom personality was so powerful he could sway the emotions of any jury.

Grundy agreed to take James into his office and so he set out for Nashville early in 1819. It was an exciting city for a young man on his own, ten times the size of Columbia, with paved streets, towering three-story buildings, well-stocked bookstores and a theater where translations of French plays were among the attractions. He enjoyed evenings with friends, and had a good time at the parties and social gatherings to which he was invited. But he didn't let the fun Nashville offered take his mind off his reason for being there.

As a clerk in Grundy's office, he copied documents, filed legal papers, ran courthouse errands and performed more menial chores such as filling inkwells and building the office fire on chilly mornings. His routine tasks gave him a practical knowledge of legal procedure, but his real education came from his own study of the books in Grundy's law library. He worked over them with the same energy he had shown at college, eager to learn all he could, and made careful notes of points that puzzled him so he could discuss them with Grundy. From Grundy himself, and from the cases he dramatically presented in court, James learned how to handle witnesses and impress judges and juries.

He had been in Nashville only a few months when the bubble of prosperity burst with a sudden drop in cotton prices. By late May, 1819, there was financial panic in Middle Tennessee. Throughout the nation, there had been a collapse of the post-war boom and when cotton prices fell, Tennessee's planters and merchants were thrown into bankruptcy. Even wealthy men like Sam Polk were hard hit, but the real burden of suffering was felt by smaller businessmen, farmers and home owners. Although he didn't realize it at the time, James Polk's career would rise from the political changes that financial crash was to bring. It started a dramatic revolt of the people for a greater voice in running the government.

At this time the people had little to say about the decisions of government. Nationally, the old Federalist party had collapsed after the War of 1812, so there no longer was any real two-party system. The Jeffersonians were in overwhelming control. In Tennessee, all the leading politicians claimed to be loyal to Jefferson, whatever their individual differences might be. Those in power, men of wealth and prestige, might group together to back one candidate against another, but the candidates would owe loyalty to the political groups rather than to the people. The public was expected to let the leaders decide what was best for them. Men, rather than issues, were put before the voters.

Since the early days of the republic, gold and silver coins had been recognized as the money a person had the right to demand in payment of debts. But Tennessee, along with many other states, had granted banks the right to make loans in the form of bank note certificates. The bank that issued these certificates promised it would redeem them in gold or silver specie on demand. Many of the banks multiplied their profits by granting so many loans of paper money that the total was far beyond their cash reserves. As long as times were good, few people demanded coins in exchange for the paper bank notes. But when the crash came and people wanted gold and silver, the banks were unable to give them cash immediately.

The bank notes fell in value and as confidence in the banks was shattered, creditors refused to accept paper money. Courts were flooded with hundreds of law suits. People who couldn't pay their debts in coin were forced to sell their property at a fraction of what it had been worth a few months before. Businesses went under, farms were lost, homes were seized for sale at auction. Everywhere, there was an outcry against the banks and against those in political control, a popular demand for reform, for new laws and new leaders.

Grundy was among the first to realize this meant a deep discontent that would sweep out the old political alliances between the leaders and those with wealth or special privilege, and would bring into power leaders willing to serve the interests of the common man. He announced himself as a candidate for a seat in the state legislature on a platform that promised relief to debtors. James Polk was in on the campaign from the start, learning from Grundy political lessons that were even more important to him than his education in law. Strongly opposed by the bankers and ruling politicians, Grundy was a wily and experienced campaigner. With the sense of dramatics he often used in the courtroom, he called his opponents enemies of the people and asked the people for a mandate to act for them. He won the election and then helped Polk win an appointment as clerk of the state senate.

Polk went with Grundy to Murfreesboro when the legislature began its session there in September. He was paid six dollars a day, which was two dollars more than the state senators and representatives received. Since the legislature usually met for only a month at a time, he still was able to spend most of the year studying law in Grundy's office in Nashville. Meanwhile, he had a chance to meet the state's leading men, to get acquainted with important people of all political factions, and to make himself well-known in the legislative chambers. Murfreesboro was still a small town, but it had grown since Polk went there to the academy. Its citizens had raised a special tax to rebuild the courthouse. Then they had induced the legislature to meet there for the first time in the vain hope that the town, which was centrally located, might be chosen the state capital.

James kept the senate journal and also saw to it that the various bills, resolutions and committee reports were carried back and forth between the two houses or sent on to the governor for signing. It was a highly responsible job and he performed it well, but he also had plenty of time for an inside view of the sessions. Some of the law makers were rough tobacco-spitting frontiersmen who kept their hats on and slouched back in their seats with their boots on the desks. The language he heard was sometimes as rough as the men. But they had their own ideas of their patriotic duty and their debates taught him much about shrewd political strategy.

Returning to Nashville when the session ended, he worked through the fall and winter to complete his law studies with Grundy and in June, 1820, appeared before the Circuit Court at Columbia and was formally admitted to the bar. His first case was to defend his own father, who had lost his temper in an argument with another man. The judge, probably amused by the situation, let Sam Polk off with a one-dollar fine. Sam also put up the money to build his son a one-room law office near Columbia's public square and to buy him a second-hand set of law books.

James Polk hung out his shingle and went to work to make his reputation as a lawyer. Most of his early cases were collecting debts for five-dollar fees, but with the help of relatives he soon began to handle land title disputes. The hearings before the Maury County Court attracted a good audience of townspeople and farmers who came for a day's free entertainment. They followed the arguments as one might a baseball game today, betting on the young lawyers who put on the best courtroom show. Polk had a chance to prove he was a good public speaker and to make his personality known. He took in another young lawyer, Madison Caruthers, as a partner, but their combined earnings the first year amounted to less than a thousand dollars.

When he returned to Murfreesboro as senate clerk for a brief special session of the legislature, some of his friends urged him to run for election himself, but he decided he wasn't ready. He wanted to wait until he was better known and the political situation was changing so fast he didn't want to commit himself to one faction or another. Rather than risk an early defeat that might put an end to his career, he decided to seek another term as senate clerk and was unanimously chosen to continue that job at the regular session in 1821.

Meanwhile his law business was growing and he began to take more cases before the Superior Court. The court held hearings in Columbia at certain times of the year and then the judge moved on around a circuit of other towns in neighboring counties. Polk followed the circuit, riding his horse from town to town with the rest of the lawyers who had business before the court, sharing tavern rooms and meals with them at the various county seats. His sense of humor and talent for telling amusing stories when they relaxed together in the evenings won him the friendship of many men who were to help him in later years. He enjoyed the jokes and also added to his practical knowledge of law by talking over points that were won or lost during the day in court. As far as politics were concerned, there were no better-posted men than the lawyers who rode the circuit.

When he and Caruthers added up their fees for the second year, they had more than doubled. Polk also had other earnings. Searching out titles, locating the holders of old land warrants, helping his family to buy up choice property that would boom in value, he became a considerable land owner himself. He was paid in land for some of his legal services and his father took him into partnership in several other land ventures.

In 1821, Grandfather Ezekiel, then a patriarch of seventy-four, pulled up stakes and led some of the family with him to still another newly-opened frontier in the western part of the state. Ezekiel prospered there during the last three years of his life, built a huge estate, and before his death in August, 1824, composed his own epitaph, painted on durable wood because "there is no rock in this country fit for grave stones." He asked that it be placed upright at his head "and a weeping willow planted at my feet." Ezekiel wrote of himself that his youthful days had been spent in pleasure, "his latter days in gathering treasure." But while he still lived, he encouraged Sam Polk to organize a surveying company for the new land, an enterprise that earned him as much as half of each tract and added thousands of new acres to the Polk domains. While James had only a small part in the operation, he also profited.

However, it was on a trip to Ezekiel's last frontier in 1821 that Sam Polk suffered an illness from which he never fully recovered. Doctors couldn't seem to find any cure for the returning attacks of fever that would come and go, confining him to his home for months at a time. Despite his father's illness, the home life James enjoyed, living with his family in that sometimes crowded house in Columbia, was close and affectionate. As the oldest of the brothers, he was able to give Franklin, and later Marshall, good first-hand advice when they were sent off to college at Chapel Hill. When his sister, Naomi, was old enough, she was sent to an academy in Nashville, and James missed her at home. But among them all, his favorites were the youngest, William and Samuel. They adored their big brother, except when he was called on to punish them or to send them dragging off to bed.

He was well-liked in Nashville and Murfreesboro and was spoken of as a "good fellow" by those who knew him at home. His popularity in Columbia won his election as captain of the cavalry regiment. Several of the town's pretty girls apparently tried to marry him, although none seemed to hold his romantic interest for long. One, whom a friend referred to in a letter as speaking his name with "wonted sweetness," pined for him in a way that "if you could but know—would wring sighs from you."

However, his mind was on other matters when he went back to Murfreesboro to take up his duties again as senate clerk at the legislative session in 1822. For one thing, his law partnership with Caruthers wasn't going well and, even though they remained friendly, Polk had found himself doing more than his share of the work. He had become acquainted with Aaron Brown, also a young lawyer and a state senator from nearby Giles County. Brown had gone to the University of North Carolina shortly before Polk and in Murfreesboro they got to be good friends. Polk wanted Brown as his partner and Brown agreed that together they could draw clients from the two counties. The matter finally was settled. Polk ended his partnership with Caruthers and started a new one with Brown.

Politically, he had reached the point where he lacked only some final spark of encouragement to put himself before the voters. Grundy had disappointed him by not making a stronger stand against paper money and by not demanding more relief for farmers and small merchants who were deeply in debt. The voters had shown their power by bringing in a complete new leadership which favored forcing the banks to redeem their notes in gold and silver coin. Polk felt it was time to make his own bid for office, but he still hesitated to announce himself as a candidate.

He found the encouragement he needed when he did fall in love. In Murfreesboro, he had renewed his friendship with the Childress family and had discovered that Sarah Childress had grown into a charming and decidedly attractive young lady. While he had been completing his studies at Chapel Hill, she had attended the best girls' school in the south, at Salem, North Carolina, until she was forced to return home by her father's death. Well-educated, accomplished in music and art, elegantly dressed and surrounded by wealth, Sarah Childress would have quickened any man's ambition.

All her life, she had been accustomed to the society of the most prominent families in the state. There was hardly a person of any importance in Tennessee who had not been entertained at some time in the splendidly furnished Childress' home. Andrew Jackson had been her father's intimate friend. For his political future, James Polk couldn't have made a better choice. But it was also the choice of his heart.

Sarah's sister Susan, already married to Doctor William Rucker, encouraged the match, and so did her mother. Polk began making the fifty-mile trip from Columbia to Murfreesboro frequently to court Sarah, even when the legislature wasn't in session. He told her about his ambition for a career in public life and Sarah, who had fallen as much in love with him, gave him the confidence he needed with her belief in him.

"She never would have married me," he said jokingly

in later years, "if I had remained only a clerk of the state senate."

But his desire to prove himself to her was no joke to him then. With an understanding between them that marriage would wait until after the coming year's election, James Polk announced that he would be a candidate from Maury County for a seat in the Tennessee House of Representatives in 1823.

Chapter Five

JAMES POLK'S first campaign for public office put him up against a veteran member of the legislature. It wasn't easy for an untried young man to win approval in those days of rough frontier electioneering. There were no clearly established political parties and no great issues to battle over with his opponent. The contest was based on personalities. He had to convince the voters he was a good fellow who would work harder to promote the interests of Maury County than the man who had been doing the job.

Sarah hardly saw him for weeks at a time as he rode his horse over the dirt roads from one village to the next and took to stump speaking in every clearing where a few settlers were willing to gather. He crossed long distances between widely separated farms to shake the hand of each neighborhood leader and try to win his support. As the race reached its climax, he was in the saddle for hours at a stretch. He ate on the run, slept when and where he could, rode for miles in sweltering sun and slogged through mud in pouring rains.

The race was close and the balloting went on for two days. At the polling places, each man entitled to a vote walked up to a table and declared his choice in public. There was nothing secret about it. No rules kept friends of one candidate or another from using last-minute threats or flattery to change a voter's mind. Liquor flowed freely and fist fights were frequent. Men gathered around to catch each arriving voter by the arm and lead him aside for a final appeal. As each vote was cast, they cheered or booed the voter, welcomed him to their circle or turned their backs upon him, as the case might be. When the poll books finally were closed and the results added up throughout the county, Polk had won by a fair majority.

Sarah was proud of him, but as glad as he was that it was over. She welcomed him happily to Murfreesboro a few days before the session was to begin in late September. While he had been campaigning, she had been busy, too, gathering her trousseau and choosing materials for her wedding gown. Polk found old friends among the law makers, but nearly as many newcomers, swept into office as he had been by the political unrest of the times.

For years, the state had been under the control of a faction headed by banker John Overton, a lawyer, planter, and land speculator and reputedly the wealthiest man in Tennessee. But the people's revolt against the old alliance of special interests and their demand for a real voice in government had brought William Carroll into power as governor. Carroll, a military hero, had been a prospering Nashville merchant during the state's inflationary boom years. Now he was a victim of the financial panic that had brought so many other merchants to ruin. Blaming the depression on the Overton group and the banks it controlled, Carroll was strongly supported by farmers, laborers, and the foes of land speculation and paper money.

Polk took his seat in the legislature faced with a decision that meant the risk of his political future. The lines were clearly drawn for a showdown battle. He would have to declare himself on the side of the conservatives or the reformers, the men of great power and influence or the common people. There was much speculation about what decision the newly-elected representative from Maury Country would make, but the Overton group felt certain he would support them since they were his own kind.

After all, they assured themselves, the Polks had always been part of the Overton alliance, sharing in the fruits of its political power. They had become people of wealth, of big business, and hardly anybody in Tennessee had gained more from land speculations. Polk himself was a land-owner, his father a director of one of the Overton banks, and his friends were their friends. Polk was a college graduate, a young gentleman, prominent in society, not the sort to throw in his lot with the "uneducated rabble." His family background as well as his upbringing reflected the advantages he had enjoyed.

But Polk had a greater political faith. It went back to his childhood in North Carolina, to the patriots of the Revolution and their struggle for freedom. It was based on that simple way of life he had known as a boy, when respect was to be won by a man's own labor and not from paper profits. From his father and Grandfather Ezekiel, he had learned to make a hero of Thomas Jefferson and to despise those who used public office for power and prestige and who favored government rule over the individual rights of man. He was no blind idealist who considered either money or the making of it evil, but he felt no loyalty to any class or political group was bigger than his obligation to the voters. Elected by the people, he considered himself a servant of those who had elected him, bound to carry out their wishes as best he could. He also sensed, more clearly than the Overton men, the direction in which the political winds were blowing and decided the time had come to take a firm stand.

Governor Carroll's message to the legislature outlined a broad program of reforms. As soon as the house was organized, Polk offered a motion to appoint special committees to consider the governor's proposals. It was a bold move for a freshman member to make, but it carried, and Polk left no doubt as to which side he had taken. Despite the fact that it was his first term, he soon was recognized as the leader of the Carroll forces in the house. Among those who backed him in the heated debates was Davy Crockett, champion of the squatters who were being driven out of their cabins in the western part of the state by owners of the spreading cotton plantations.

But Polk found himself in the unhappy position of having to battle Felix Grundy. The man who had given him his law education and first training in politics, who had made Polk his protégé and helped him become clerk of the senate, was now his chief opponent. Grundy had done a political about-face and decided he had less to gain from the reform group than from the conservatives and was back in the Overton camp. He argued that the bankers couldn't redeem their paper notes for gold and silver coin without calling in so many loans that even more debtors would be ruined.

Polk and Crockett attacked the argument as a weak excuse and declared that the whole Overton-controlled banking system was nothing but "swindling on a large scale." Grundy then worked up a bill that seemed to provide for gold and silver payments but was so cleverly worded it actually would have let the banks avoid making them. He tried to rush the measure through before its meaning was clearly understood, but Polk challenged him.

Jumping to his feet, Polk made a motion to table Grundy's bill until it had been fully discussed. Grundy protested that it was the usual procedure to pass a bill for its first reading and then argue its merits. Polk answered that he was aware that the bill was Grundy's "favorite child," which the bankers were trying to "nourish and raise to manhood," but that it was such a dangerous measure it should be "arrested at the threshold." He exposed it as a hidden attempt to repeal the Specie Resumption Act and declared that any further delay in paying off bank notes with hard money would depreciate their value so much as to wreck the state's currency.

Polk's attack aroused his fellow law makers to the real meaning of the measure and they approved his motion to table it. But that was only the start of the debates that went on for days between Grundy and Polk. Grundy turned against him all the oratorical skill that Polk had so much admired when he had listened to him sway courtroom juries and capture campaign audiences. Playing on the emotions of members of the legislature, Grundy painted a picture of suffering and dire poverty if the banks were forced to call in their loans to meet the demands for payment in coin. But Polk used Grundy's own methods to warn that if specie payments failed it would be "calamitous to the people." He cited acts of the British parliament to back his opinion and when Grundy questioned him on points of law, he was able to prove his former instructor wrong.

They also clashed over land reform measures that brought Polk into conflict not only with Grundy and the

Overton group, but also with the University of North Carolina which claimed some Tennessee property under old grants to soldiers of the Revolution. Grundy argued that Tennessee's honor would be at stake if it failed to approve the old claims. Warning his listeners against "the charm of Mr. Grundy's eloquence," Polk objected that they couldn't go on forever recognizing grants made years before statehood. He argued that instead of selling them to speculators for money that would go to the university, the lands should be sold by Tennessee to develop public schools of its own.

Some of his friends at Chapel Hill accused him of disloyalty to his alma mater, and others in North Carolina, including his own relatives, pleaded with him to change his mind. But Polk stood by his principles. The vote was a close one, but Grundy was defeated. Polk then went on, not only to condemn private appropriation of the lands, but to demand that other property, to which the federal government still held title, should be ceded to Tennessee for the school fund. He was appointed chairman of a committee to draft a memorial to Congress for that purpose.

The outraged Overton men, fearing an end to future land speculation in the state's western district, carried their own pleas to Washington. They also managed to arouse the legislature of North Carolina to send a complaint to Congress protesting the actions that Tennessee had taken under Polk's leadership. As a result, Congress delayed any immediate decision.

When the question of supporting a federal survey for a national road from Buffalo to New Orleans came up, Polk and Grundy were at odds again. Although Polk generally was against the spending of any large sums of the taxpayers' money on extensive road-building projects, he favored a national road that would go through Tennessee. Denouncing Grundy for trying to protect the interests of the private turnpike owners instead of the public good, Polk was put on a committee to petition Congress to make the survey.

He led a move for tax reform, so land owners would be taxed according to the true value of their property, and successfully fought for a reduction of poll taxes. With Davy Crockett, he argued for a change in divorce laws, so that poor people would be able to take such cases into court rather than obtain divorce by a special act of the legislature, a procedure usually available only to the wealthy. Polk also favored changing some of the penal laws and abolishing imprisonment for debt.

Even though he was a leader of the Carroll forces, he frequently took an independent stand against legislation the governor wanted. With a toughness of character that sometimes surprised his friends as much as his opponents, he voted against the Carroll group on bills that conflicted with his own beliefs. He had chosen the side of the reformers to fight for the democratic principles that were his faith.

He soon was faced with a dilemma that went far beyond local issues, when Andrew Jackson made his first bid for the Presidency. There were no national conventions to nominate candidates for President and Vice President in those days. Nominations were made by the members of Congress, who met in caucus to choose the candidates. But throughout the country, there had been growing opposition to the idea of letting Congress name the men who would be put before the voters. Legislatures in various states also made nominations, by passing resolutions to name candidates they hoped other states might decide to back. At other political gatherings, whenever the opportunity presented itself, a toast might be offered to nominate someone for the Presidency.

Outstanding men in each state, who hoped to start a movement that would win the support of groups in other states, often arranged to have their names suggested several years before the actual election, so the campaign would have a chance to grow. As soon as one President was inaugurated, the race would be on among possible successors. The national election was still a year away when Jackson's candidacy presented a more immediate problem for Polk. Grundy and the Overton men had started the Jackson boom in the hope of riding in on his popularity to regain their own power in the state. Polk, as an ardent supporter of the Carroll forces, was against most things Jackson's backers stood for, but strongly in favor of the man himself.

Jackson had been his father's friend and his own hero, but Polk's belief in him went deeper than the hero worship which had surrounded the General since the Battle of New Orleans. From everything Jackson said and did, he seemed to Polk a true champion of his own democratic ideals. Jackson was gaining support throughout the nation, from the laborers of Philadelphia, the frontiersmen of Mississippi, the democratic farmers in other states. He was winning a strength from the people themselves that was making even the old-line Tennessee politicians who had backed him uncomfortable. Many of them had no real desire to see Jackson made President. They secretly favored Henry Clay or John Quincy Adams and intended to use Jackson's popularity with the people of Tennessee to help themselves.

Their immediate goal in 1823 was to put their own man in the United States Senate by keeping the legislature from re-electing the Carroll man, John Williams.

But Williams had such strength that the politicians finally decided only Jackson himself could beat him. They put Jackson's name before the legislature for election to the federal Senate. Polk, in order to help Jackson win, was torn between supporting Governor Carroll and John Williams or siding with the very group he had been fighting against. Jackson's friends were not too sure that even he could defeat Williams. If he lost his bid for a seat in the Senate, was beaten in that contest in his own state, his chances for the presidency might be destroyed.

Polk's influence, as a leader of the Carroll faction, could win Jackson the slim margin of votes he needed. With political courage, Polk decided to go over to the opposition and took an independent stand for Jackson. Davy Crockett and most of the Carroll party stood by Williams when the vote was counted, but there were enough who were with Polk to win Jackson's place in the Senate, and thus save his chance for the Presidency, by only ten votes.

For Polk's own future, the decision was among the most important he ever made. Jackson never forgot that Polk, instead of making an easy choice, had opposed his own group in order to back him. Grateful to Polk for helping to save his political career, Jackson became his close personal and political friend. Polk said in later years that few acts of his life had given him greater pride.

On New Year's day, 1824, Sarah Childress became Mrs. James Polk at a large country wedding held in her mother's home near Murfreesboro. Polk's old school teacher, Parson Henderson, performed the Presbyterian ceremony and his law partner, Aaron Brown, was best man. One of his North Carolina cousins, Lucius Polk, who also was an attendant at the wedding, wrote home to say that "James is one of the first young men in the state." The affair, which was a major social event in Tennessee, drew friends from Nashville, Columbia, and more distant places, and the guests included Jackson's adopted nephew, Andrew Jackson Donelson, who later would negotiate the annexation of Texas.

The newlyweds began a round of parties and receptions, climaxed by a gala entertainment given in their honor by Sarah's sister, Mrs. Rucker, in Murfreesboro. Because of poor roads and midwinter floods, it took them most of a week to travel the fifty miles to Columbia and they spent one night in a farm cabin on the way, waiting for a river to lower enough to ford it with their carriage. In Columbia, Polk's mother introduced the twenty-year-old bride to her new relatives and neighbors at a party attended by nearly the whole town.

One of the guests commented in a letter that Sarah wasn't strikingly beautiful, but that she had an attractive personality, wit, grace, a charming social manner, and was "an intelligent and animated conversationalist." Polk, who was some eight years her senior, was described as a very youthful-looking and happy bridegroom, and the neighbors generally agreed that they made a handsome and well-suited couple.

They moved into a rented cottage for a while and then into a house of their own across the street from his parents' place, a modest two-story home with a separate kitchen and smokehouse in the rear yard. Sarah enjoyed entertaining his friends and there were plenty of relatives to keep her company. She became a favorite of Polk's mother, and as an equally devout Presbyterian was welcomed into the activities of Columbia's new church where

Polk bought them a pew. On the Sundays that he was home, Sarah encouraged him to attend services with the family.

But Polk's political life often took him away from home. His prominence in the legislature and his close ties with Jackson had started talk about sending him to Congress. During the spring and summer of 1824, he had many meetings with leaders of various factions, including Grundy, and by August had announced himself as a candidate for election from the Sixth Congressional District, made up of Bedford, Lincoln, and Giles Counties as well as his own Maury County.

The Congressional election wouldn't be held until the following year, but meanwhile there was the campaign to elect Jackson President. The Tennessee politicians who had nominated Jackson mainly to serve their own cause in the state had seen his popularity catch on across the country until they were forced to accept the fact that there really might be a chance he would become the nation's chief executive. Belatedly, and perhaps with some misgivings over the democratic uprising they had created, they decided on an all-out fight to win him the election. Polk needed no urging to champion his favorite. He was so active in Jackson's campaign, and in planning his own race for Congress which was to follow it, that he had little time left for his law practice. He and Brown, although still the closest of friends, decided to end their partnership and Polk carried on the reduced law business alone.

In addition to Jackson, state legislatures and mass meetings had nominated John Quincy Adams, Henry Clay, and John Calhoun for President. Calhoun decided to drop out after he had been promised backing for the Vice Presidency which he was surer of winning. Meanwhile, members of Congress had met in caucus and officially nominated William Crawford, who had been Madison's Secretary of War and Monroe's Secretary of the Treasury. But the system of having Congress nominate a candidate had grown so unpopular that only about one-fourth of the members took part in the caucus. It was the last time the caucus method was used. Political parties were developing and at the next election they would make nominations at their national conventions.

As election day approached, Crawford was all but put out of the race by illness. But he still held enough electoral votes to throw the contest into doubt. Polk was greatly disappointed when the battle in which he had fought so hard failed to give Jackson a clear victory. Jackson won the greatest number of the nation's electoral votes, 99 to 84 for Adams, but neither of them had a majority. Crawford took 41 of the electoral votes and Clay had 37.

Under the Constitution, the election was thrown into the House of Representatives, where the members were to decide which of the three top contenders would be President. As the lowest man, Clay was eliminated from the voting, but as Speaker and boss of the House he was in a position to influence its outcome and he gave his support to Adams. On February 9, 1825, the House chose Adams instead of Jackson as President and when Adams appointed Clay as his Secretary of State, Polk joined in the cry of Jackson men throughout the country that a "corrupt bargain" had been made.

Thousands of voters, including nearly all Jackson's followers, thought they had been cheated and that there was something wrong with an election system that would let Congress overthrow the will of the people. The uproar, in addition to boosting Jackson's popularity as a man who had been "done wrong," helped put an end to the system of nominating candidates by Congress. But even after the national conventions began to nominate candidates, state legislatures continued to offer the names of men they considered possibilities. This was done partly in the hope of influencing the party choices at the national conventions. And candidates for President still began bids for office years before the election.

For Jackson, there would be another chance at the Presidency in the next national election, but Polk was more determined than ever to win a seat in Congress where he could work to vindicate Jackson. His chief opponent in the congressional district was an old foe of Jackson's, Andrew Erwin, who could do the General's cause much harm in Washington. But Polk wasn't Erwin's only opponent. Three other Jackson supporters also had entered the race against Erwin and it looked as though the Jackson vote might be so badly split Erwin would get in.

Early in May, James and Sarah journeyed to Nashville for a huge celebration that drew 25,000 people from all parts of Tennessee to honor Lafayette, the great French patriot general and friend of the American colonies, who was visiting the United States. The hotels were overrun with guests and the Polks stayed at the home of their friend, Judge John Catron of the State Supreme Court. Sarah, who loved the excitement of social affairs, enjoyed every minute of the parades and military reviews, the gala balls and elaborate formal dinners.

But for Polk, the celebration offered more than entertainment. The invitations had struck the political keynote of the event by picturing a bust of Lafayette on one side and a matching bust of Jackson on the other, linking their heroism with the listed dates of their victorious battles between entwined columns that were surrounded by drawings of cannon balls, drums, and torches. Their design was the work of Ralph Earle, Jackson's artist friend and companion, who lived with him at the Hermitage. In paying honor to Lafayette, Tennesseeans were not being allowed to forget they had an illustrious hero of their own. Polk, as a Jackson man, made the most of the opportunity to become better known to important people beyond his own part of the state.

It was a working vacation for Polk, but one of the few chances he would have to spend much time with Sarah for weeks to come. He plunged into the active campaign for a seat in Congress with all the odds against him. A friend of those times, a fellow-lawyer and neighbor, A. O. P. Nicholson, wrote: "The chances at the outset were decidedly against him, but he had his heart set upon success and he resolved to attain it. The district was large, but he traversed and canvassed it again and again .... In his public speeches there was always an earnestness and sincerity of manner which was peculiarly impressive .... This was the secret of his success as a popular orator. He was persuasive because he spoke from his heart as well as from his head."

Before the campaign was half over, the four other candidates knew Polk was the man they had to beat. Three of them claimed the same political faith and even Erwin slanted his speeches in an attempt to win some of the pro-Jackson votes. As the election battle neared its end, according to Nicholson, Polk displayed "all the skill of a veteran general in marshalling his forces" and "dashed from point to point over his district with a rapidity which struck his opponents with surprise and ... infused his own friends with the same ardor and energy which actuated himself."

Polk defeated Erwin by less than a thousand votes out of more than ten thousand cast, but the three other contenders trailed and he had a clear victory. In the seven years since he had graduated from college, he had become one of the state's most successful young lawyers, a leader of the legislature, accepted into the councils of Tennessee's most prominent and powerful men, and now had beaten a dangerous political enemy of Andrew Jackson's. He was on his way to Washington, where he would help to direct the national campaign to put Jackson into the White House, and to take his seat in a Congress that was about to pay considerable attention to James Knox Polk.

Chapter Six

CONGRESSMAN-ELECT James Polk set off for Washington on horseback in the fall of 1825 with the personal blessing of Andrew Jackson, who had visited Columbia to wish him well. Several other Tennessee Congressmen joined him at Nashville and they made the long ride up across Kentucky and eastward through the mountains together. At Baltimore they arranged to have their horses cared for until their return the following spring and took the stagecoach into Washington over a bumpy and twisting dirt road.

Washington was still a town of streets clouded with blowing dust in summer and soggy with ankle-deep mud in winter. Its plainly constructed public buildings were spaced out with wide gaps between them according to the grand plan for a city which had yet to grow. Along Pennsylvania Avenue, from the low-domed Capitol to the President's Mansion, was a motley row of shops, stables, boarding houses, drinking and gambling places, and a few hotels. In the square before the Capitol, there were piles of stone and other building materials to complete the reconstruction that had followed its burning by the British during their wartime occupation eleven years before. Polk moved into Captain Benjamin Burch's boarding house on Capitol Hill, where he had his own room for sleeping and an office. He shared meals at a common mess table with a large group of other Congressmen.

While he was on his way to Washington, the stage had been set for the battle to make Jackson President in 1828. Jackson had resigned his seat in the Senate and the Tennessee legislature had renominated him for the Presidency that was three years away. When the Nineteenth Congress began its first session in December, 1825, both houses were firmly in control of incoming President John Quincy Adams and his Secretary of State, Henry Clay, but a challenge was already in the making. Polk was among the small group of Jackson men in open opposition at the start of the Congressional session. From the beginning, he placed himself squarely on the side of a people's government against those who believed with equal sincerity that the "upper classes" of property, business, wealth, and high education should decide what was best for the people rather than let a common majority rule.

He was honestly shocked by the philosophy of Adams and Clay, and for him it was a crusade of faith against men he considered dangerous enemies of democracy. They, in turn, felt that Polk and his kind would wreck the nation by destroying the power of Congress to nominate or perhaps choose the President. They also opposed Polk's acceptance of the will of the people instead of the reasoned judgment of the elite. Polk found himself at the center of a historic controversy that was to become an angry storm before his fourteen years in Congress ended.

But on his first day, the battle was still being fought behind the scenes in the conferences that Jackson men were holding with other enemies of the Adams' administration. In the Hall of the House of Representatives, he took his chosen seat in one of the semi-circular rows that faced the Speaker's desk, where blazing fireplaces at each side provided the room's only heat. The Hall was poorly designed for public speaking, with troublesome acoustics that produced trick echoes and sometimes reduced a speaker's words to a whisper that couldn't be heard clearly a few feet away. But as Polk looked around him, and up at the crowded visitors' galleries, he was deeply impressed and perhaps slightly awed by the knowledge of the great voices that had spoken there.

Most of his work during the early part of the session was the routine duty of any new Representative. As a newcomer, and also one of the body's younger members, he had to win the confidence of the older and more experienced leaders and meanwhile make sure he satisfied the voters back home. He made himself a record book by fastening together sheets of writing paper and binding them into a cover simply marked, "Congress, U.S." Day by day, on its note-sized pages, Polk carefully entered a record of the endless little time-consuming tasks he performed as the Washington servant of his constituents in Tennessee.

He filed pension petitions for them, entered land claim papers, paid a dollar out of his own pocket for a map one of his voters wanted, forwarded fees to the patent office, and spoke to the Secretary of War about a Tennesseean who was trying to collect his back pay as an army officer. Night after night, he sat in his boarding house room, penning the expected personal replies to those who made demands on his services. He investigated a claim for indemnity on property seized years before by the Indians, collected funds for a mail carrier, and tried to placate an angry individual who wanted the government to pay him for a horse lost during the war.

Polk answered every request, no matter how unimportant it seemed, and he also kept up a heavy personal correspondence with political friends in his district. One of them, Jim White, complained that newspapers weren't saying much about Polk and that he should write to everybody he knew and spread the news of his activities. He also advised him to make some "thundering speeches." But during his first few months in Congress, Polk was given little opportunity to be heard. Until Adams was inaugurated in March, Congress marked time on most matters of importance. With the House under the control of Adams and Clay, the leaders deliberately ignored Polk, as a Jackson man, in making important committee appointments.

He found it almost as difficult at first, despite his personal friendship and constant exchange of letters with Jackson, to win more than a minor part in the President-making strategy being planned by the Jackson group in Washington. Although Polk was described by one of the group as "the cleverest man in the delegation," it took him a while to impress Senator John Eaton, Jackson's personal campaign manager. But he gradually gained the confidence of the Jackson leaders and proved his devotion to the cause by becoming one of the financial backers of a Jackson newspaper in Washington, the *United States Telegraph*. He worked with Eaton to strengthen the faltering paper by bringing in hard-hitting Duff Green as owner and editor. Polk endorsed the note that enabled Green to buy it.

The Jacksonians went to work to unite all the enemies of the administration behind their cause. They won the powerful support of Vice President John Calhoun and his friends, who wanted Clay out of the way to improve Calhoun's chance of becoming President later. New York's

Senator Martin Van Buren also gave them a sympathetic hearing. All sorts of forces banded together in their fear that the administration was trying to revive the old Federalist policies. When President Adams made his inaugural address in March, including in it a caution to Congressmen against being "palsied by the will of our constituents," he brought into the open many of the issues that had been a festering source of discontent.

Drawn together by Polk and the other Jackson leaders, the opponents of Adams and Clay began a fighting attack that hit the administration on every issue brought to the floor and they repeated the constant charge that it held power because of a "corrupt bargain" that had thwarted the people's will. Less than two weeks after Adams took his oath of office, Polk made his first major speech in the House with a demand that the electoral college be abolished so the people could vote directly for President.

He knew there was little chance that the Constitutional amendment he called for would be adopted. But it gave him an opportunity to present a clear challenge that would help arouse the people. In making it, Polk set forth the basic views of direct government by the people that he was to champion for the rest of his political life. He denounced the choice of Presidents by members of the House, declaring that a President was the chief magistrate of the whole people and should be dependent upon them alone. Polk added that the Representatives themselves enjoyed no power of their own, but were merely delegates of the people, bound to "obey the instructions of those who send them here."

"That this is a government based on the will of the people; that all power emanates from them; and that a majority should rule," he said, "are, as I conceive, vital principles in this government, never to be sacrificed or abandoned under any circumstance."

In the debate that followed, the scholarly Edward Everett from Massachusetts made a direct thrust at Jackson by warning that if the government ever were destroyed "it would not be by a President elected by a minority of the people, but by a President elected by an overwhelming majority of the people, by some military chieftain that should rise in the land."

"Yes, sir," Polk shot back, "by some 'military chieftain' whose only crime it was to have served his country faithfully at a period when that country needed and realized his services." Turning from Everett to look at the other administration leaders, he added that there were those who were continually in alarm "lest the people should destroy the government," but that the truth was that the government was in far more danger from an administration that lacked the people's support than from "all the ideal dangers which the gentlemen seem to apprehend are covertly lurking among the great body of the people of the Union."

His proposed Constitutional amendment was referred to a special committee, of which Polk was made a member, but it was bottled up there by Adams' men who had no intention of letting any such "dangerous ideas" come back to the floor for further debate. Polk wasn't too disappointed because printed copies of his speech and of the revealing debates, including his remarks about Jackson, were widely circulated. Jackson wrote him a note of congratulation and added that the speech had been well-received in Tennessee and would help him with his own constituents.

In his writings, Polk usually capitalized the word "People," and when he was debating against what he considered unnecessary federal projects, he often referred to government appropriations as "the People's money." He insisted on calling Congressmen "People's representatives" and warned that they should never be "mere passive agents to record the decrees of the President."

The problem of slavery, which was brought into several debates during the session, was one that troubled him throughout his career, both as a person and a public leader, because he feared it would tear the nation apart. He accepted it as a situation that existed when the country became independent, "entailed upon us by our ancestors," but it was one for which he never found a solution that he believed would be both practical and humane. As a southerner, raised in the slave-owning tradition, he was more liberal than some Tennesseans of his time. Considering slaves different from all other kinds of property in that "they were rational, they were human beings," he never defended the principle of slavery, but never took a stand against what he felt he couldn't change.

Polk devoted much of his time in the first session to carrying on the fight he had started in the Tennessee legislature to get the government to cede federal lands in the western district of the state to endow a fund for a public school system. He managed to get his bill to the floor, but administration leaders finally had it tabled without a vote.

When Congress adjourned late in May, Polk hurried home to be with Sarah and to mend his political fences. He spent a good part of the summer conferring with state leaders and renewing the friendship of voters in his district by taking part in militia musters and other public affairs. Deeply saddened by the death of his boyhood idol, Thomas Jefferson, on the fiftieth anniversary of independence, July 4, 1826, Polk solemnly called attention to "the present crisis of affairs" in a talk he made a short time later at a dinner of the militia regiment of which he had become colonel.

Declaring that "the issue is joined" between the power of the administration and the rights of the people, he called upon those attending the day-long gathering to join him in the hope that the Constitution might "survive the shock in its original republican simplicity and purity" and that the people's victory in electing their next President might be a triumph as great "as it was glorious in 1801, on the ascension of that venerable patriot Thomas Jefferson to the Presidential chair."

Sarah was determined to go back with her husband when he returned to Washington, and Polk was just as eager to take her after the loneliness of his enforced "bachelorhood" at the capital. They turned the trip into something of a vacation, despite the tiring journey over rough roads, by making it in their own comfortable carriage, accompanied by a maid and a manservant. Congressman Sam Houston joined them at Nashville and Senator Hugh White, a former president of the state bank and judge of the Tennessee Supreme Court, became a member of the party when they reached Knoxville.

Stopping at farmhouses along the way, often cooking their meals over open fires in the woods, they made the trip in leisurely stages, enjoying the outdoors and the scenic beauty. Sarah wrote to her relatives about her adventures crossing the undeveloped lands, fording rivers, and going through deep forests that had been Indian hunting grounds, and poetically described how the golden sunshine and brilliant colors of October gradually changed to the soft silvery haze of November in the wildwood solitudes. When they reached Washington, they spent a few days at Williamson's Hotel while they were hunting for a place to live, since it was unusual even for Congressmen who brought their wives to rent homes of their own.

They finally found quarters at a boarding house on Pennsylvania Avenue, where they shared the dinner table and common parlor with Congressional families from eight other states. The arrangement gave Sarah congenial company and they had many visitors, including the handsome lawyer and author, Francis Scott Key, whom the ladies privately called "Mr. Star Spangled Banner."

Sarah took up the piano again for awhile, but the dinners, parties, and formal balls in which she delighted kept her so busy she found little time for her music. Before long, she was among the most popular young wives in the Congressional set and the Polks were being invited everywhere. This not only made Sarah happy but also was a considerable help to Polk in meeting the important people who could further his career. While Sarah seldom joined the men in their discussion of politics, she became quite expert on the subjects being debated in Congress and on the changes in political alliance that were so much part of the talk in the capital's drawing rooms. When her husband spoke in the House, she was always in the visitors' gallery, proudly listening and ready to praise him afterwards or offer criticism. He teased her sometimes over the fact that with her ears attuned to Washington gossip she often learned of political trends before he did.

Polk launched an attack in the House against the administration's control of Congress through the committee system. Although he finally had won a minor assignment himself, to the Committee on Public Expenditures, he accused the Adams and Clay forces of arranging the committees to "sustain an administration which never came into power by the voice of the people." The opposition was growing stronger and his fortunes were rising with it. Back in Tennessee, Jackson was paying increasing attention to the news and political advice Polk included in his letters and told him that he welcomed his suggestions. In his own letters to others in Washington, Jackson often mentioned Polk.

But there was also bad news from home, both personal and political, for the Polks that winter. His father's health was failing rapidly and the doctors gave little hope for his recovery. On the political scene, Lunsford Bramlett, one of the candidates Polk had defeated to win his place in Congress, had already begun a campaign to beat him in the coming August election. Bramlett seemed likely to get the support of the old Erwin faction in one county, had gathered strength in another, and was spending his full time attacking Polk throughout the rest of the district. He had devoted an entire month to the effort in Polk's home county of Maury alone and Polk's friends were so worried some wrote him that his chances of returning to Congress seemed mighty slim.

He and Sarah made the trip back to Columbia as fast as they could after Congress adjourned in March. By the time they reached there, his father's condition had become so alarming the family was resigned to his death. Under heavy sedation to ease his pain, Sam Polk's mind wandered, and there were sad days when he failed to recognize his son. But in the fleeting moments of clarity, Sam himself realized the end was coming and to please Polk's mother, asked to become a member of the Presbyterian church. For hopeless days, all through the hot summer, Sam clung to the last threads of life, his mind mostly gone.

Shocked and worried with grief, equally worried over

the ordeal it was for his mother, Polk faced the election. After a careful canvass of Bramlett's strength, he felt more confident than his friends. "I shall enter the contest as usual," he said, "and will be found at my post." But his confidence didn't keep him from making the most energetic campaign of his life. All through the spring and summer, he rode his horse into every village and town, issuing a call to the voters to rescue the republic from a crisis he considered as great as that which had faced Jefferson.

Attacking the position taken by President Adams that "Liberty is power," Polk warned that such a doctrine would lead to "despotism itself." Ridiculing the administration's "pomp, pagentry and show of European etiquette," he called for a return to "republican simplicity." He urged his listeners not to be misled by those who labeled themselves republicans while serving the special interests of aristocratic rule. "Those who are not for the People, and for popular rights, are against them," he said. But he had no doubt that, just as in Jefferson's time, the nation would be saved by that "great body of the People, the uncorrupted and incorruptible source of all power."

It was his belief in his cause more than in himself that made him sure of victory. Two weeks before the election, Erwin's son wrote to Henry Clay that "we think we will be able to beat Polk." But Polk's own confidence was confirmed. He defeated Bramlett by only 1,500 votes, but ran way ahead of the other Jackson sympathizers for state offices. Sam Houston, who had entered the same election to become governor of Tennessee, lost in two of Polk's counties, although he had enough of a majority throughout the state to elect him.

He and Sarah were getting ready to return to Washington in November when his father died. Polk inherited a major share of the large estate, including thousands of acres of land, but as the new head of the family, he also was burdened with the affairs of his younger brothers and sisters. His father was hardly in his grave before Polk's two married sisters and their husbands tried to break the will, claiming that they hadn't received a large enough share. Lydia's husband threatened to spend every cent he had to defeat Polk the next time he ran for election unless she was given more of the money. A settlement finally was worked out and friendly family relationships were restored, but the responsibility of managing the estate and trying to be a father to the younger ones was a burden for many years. One of his brothers was an alcoholic and most of the others had wild streaks that constantly involved them in troubles he tried to straighten out.

Exhausted by the campaign, his father's death, and the family troubles, Polk needed a rest, but it was urgent for him to get to Washington. Throughout the nation, the Congressional elections had proven Jackson's growing popularity by sweeping his supporters into office, and in the session about to begin John Quincy Adams would become the first President in history to face a Congress controlled by the opposition. Polk could expect greater recognition now and a larger part in the fight that remained to bring Jackson into the White House.

He and Sarah did decide to make the trip as relaxing as they could by leaving their carriage at Lexington and taking an Ohio River steamer to Wheeling, where they could get a connecting stage for the capital. They had the company of a new member of Congress, John Bell, who had defeated Felix Grundy in the Nashville district. When they reached Washington, the Polks were invited to take up quarters in a boarding house where Vice President Calhoun and his top Congressional leaders made their home. Bell also was invited to live there, as did Senator Hugh White. The Polks shared a dining table with the most prominent members of Congress and their wives were to become Sarah's friends.

When the Twentieth Congress met in December, 1827, with Jackson forces in control, Polk was appointed to the important Foreign Affairs Committee. One of the questions they considered was what to do about the little known territory of Oregon. President Adams' administration had extended an agreement with the British for continued joint occupation and there were some Jacksonians who wanted to make a campaign issue of it by demanding the building of forts, the selling of lands and the setting up of a territorial government.

Polk agreed that the United States seemed to have the best title to the area, but said the building of forts would invite war and break our solemn agreement with the British. Instead, he urged sending explorers to find out more about conditions in Oregon, and meanwhile he favored court protection for American citizens there. He managed to have the bill withdrawn and modified to fit his suggestions. When opponents tacked on the provision for building forts as an amendment, Polk helped to kill the measure rather than risk war to create a campaign issue.

Sam Houston's resignation from Congress to become governor of Tennessee meant that Jackson had to rely on Polk to supply him with the inside information about Congressional activities that Houston had been providing. Polk became Jackson's confidant in the lower house, sending him detailed reports along with advice and suggestions, and Jackson soon was writing from the Hermitage to tell other leaders that he had the highest confidence in Polk's judgment.

Polk took a leading part in defending Jackson against slanderous charges in what became one of the dirtiest election campaigns in American history. Adams and Clay supporters attacked the General as an ignorant man who could hardly read and write, a person with a scandalous private life, a bully and tyrant, and even accused him of being a murderer. They tried to blacken the reputation of Jackson's ailing wife, questioning her divorce from her first husband and her marriage to Jackson in scurrilous pamphlets which Polk did his best to contradict.

The most damaging charges, said to have been inspired by Clay himself, were in the form of black-bordered handbills which pictured the coffins of men Jackson was accused of ordering shot. The "coffin handbills," widely circulated throughout the country, claimed to give an account of "some of the bloody deeds of General Jackson." They were based on an incident of the War of 1812 when Jackson, struggling to keep his army together, had approved the court martial of six soldiers who defied their officers and deserted. Polk managed to dig up evidence that cleared Jackson of blame. He then prepared a brief account of the case which was printed in many newspapers, where it was seen by voters who hadn't read the dry Congressional report, and helped to turn the effect of the "coffin handbills" against Adams and Clay.

Hurrying home from Washington when Congress adjourned in May, 1828, Polk built up a strong Jackson organization in his own district and took to the stump in active campaigning. He had to interrupt his fight for Jackson's election to nurse Sarah through a severe attack of measles and again to inspect some of the lands his father had left him in the western part of the state, but he was back in Columbia in time to celebrate the overwhelming victory. With John Calhoun to be Vice President again, and with the backing of Martin Van Buren in New York, Jackson had been swept into office with four times the popular vote of 1824.

He and Sarah paid a brief visit to Jackson at the Hermitage on their way to Washington, taking with them Polk's sister, Ophelia, a popular young lady of sixteen. Sam Houston, who was another of Jackson's guests, apparently was quite taken with Ophelia. Tennessee's bachelor governor made note of the fact that "Miss Polk is not only a fine young lady," but also a wealthy one in her own right with "*quills* to the amount of many thousands, say $40,000." Houston, however, soon was to marry another girl and then, after a never-explained quarrel with his bride, to resign the governorship and abruptly head west to live among the Indians.

Polk was worried over Sarah's health by the time they reached Washington. Still weak from her summer's illness, she had been exhausted by the trip and was so tired one of their friends, Senator Levi Woodbury, wrote his wife that Sarah looked "as if grown 45 years older and seems awkward and distrait." But as the exultant Jacksonians prepared for Inauguration Day, she was caught up in the gay social activities. She took Ophelia along to a reception to meet outgoing President Adams and the two of them gloated a bit over his sour-faced disappointment in having lost the election. Polk, meanwhile, was busy handling arrangements for Jackson's triumphal journey to the capital.

Chapter Seven

THERE WAS hardly anybody who felt more personal pride than James Polk over the acclaim given President Andrew Jackson on that Inauguration Day, March 4, 1829. Jackson at sixty-two was haggard and ill, grief-stricken by the death of his wife since the election and by the belief that the slanders of Adams and Clay had hounded her into her grave. Still, he stood tall and lean, every inch a fighter, as he strode from the Capitol rotunda to be greeted by a great cheering shout that rose as one mighty voice from the square below.

It was the voice of the people, and Jackson's day of victory was Polk's victory, too. Farmers, laborers, and shopkeepers were the rulers-to-be, and this was their President, the first one clearly chosen by the will of the people themselves. As Polk stood behind Jackson on the east portico, he shared that jubilation. For the moment, at least, he was untroubled by wondering how the new government could satisfy the claims of all the factions that had banded together to bring it to power.

But even as Jackson rode off on horseback toward the White House at the head of the happy crowd that would storm into its parlors for a riotous celebration, the politicians were quarreling over positions of leadership. The backers of Calhoun and Van Buren were at war, others were fighting among themselves both nationally and in Tennessee, and Polk felt like a man trying to walk a tightrope across a widening political chasm with the supporting cliffs on both sides crumbling away.

With the votes of this Presidential election hardly counted, the politicians were plotting their chances in the next one, four years ahead. The Calhoun group had been confident that he as Vice President would follow Jackson into office when the time came. Jackson, however, apparently had set Van Buren on his way to the White House by making him Secretary of State and largely ignoring Calhoun men in making his top cabinet choices. Jackson's quarrel with Calhoun was to grow over many causes, both political and personal, until there was a complete break between them. Polk, with friends on both sides, was already disillusioned by the greedy eagerness to claim the spoils he saw all around him.

He was glad the adjournment of Congress soon after the inauguration let him escape to Tennessee, where he spent a restful summer at home, his popularity with the voters of his own district so great he hardly had to campaign for re-election. Putting off the return to Washington as long as possible, he and Sarah made the journey by way of an Ohio River steamboat in November and then took a short cruise from Baltimore down the Chesapeake Bay to Norfolk. But they finally had to turn back to the capital, where he faced a winter of cautiously trying to maintain friendships in a place seething with intrigue and gossip.

It had been enough before to be a Jackson man, but now every decision was a matter of loyalty either to Calhoun or Van Buren. Polk felt his principles wouldn't let him blindly follow the program of either group and was determined to stay independent. He sided with the Calhoun men on some issues and with the Van Buren forces on others. Saying it was too early to talk about who would take Jackson's place, he declared that the business at hand was to support the administration and give the people what they expected from it.

The real enemies, as he saw it, were the bankers, the powerful merchants and manufacturers, those who wanted to increase taxes and duties and the price of land and had as their spokesman Henry Clay. In the first session after Jackson became President, Polk outlined the philosophy he would follow during his whole career in Congress.

"I would sell out the public lands at low prices, at much lower prices than they have ever been sold," Polk said. "I would have them speedily settled by a hardy race of enterprising freemen, who would feel they had a stake in the Government. I would impose no unnecessary taxation upon them, to support any particular interest. I would relieve the burdens of the whole community, as far as possible, by reducing taxes. I would keep as much money in the treasury as the safety of the Government required and no more. I would leave no surplus revenue there to scramble for ... I would bring the Government back to what it was intended to be, a plain economical Government."

That summer, he and Sarah relaxed after the tension in Washington by again turning their trip home into a long vacation, visiting New York and then going up the Hudson and along the Erie Canal to do some sight-seeing at Niagara Falls. Back in Columbia, he attended a dinner in his honor and delivered a speech for free trade which brought cheers from his listeners when he declared people should be free "to sell what we have to spare in the market where we can sell it for the best price and to buy what we need in the market where we can buy it cheapest." President Jackson also came to Tennessee for part of the summer, to negotiate an Indian treaty, and Polk took his youngest brother, Sam, along to meet Jackson at the pow-wow.

But the Polks had been so unhappy in Washington the winter before that when the time came to go back, Sarah decided it would be better for her to stay home. In an atmosphere where any sign of friendship could be interpreted as having political meaning, where one group of wives snubbed another and gossip could condemn a man for the company his wife chose, Sarah had found it too trying to keep up her social activities and still do nothing that might hurt his career. She argued it would be easier for them both if he went without her.

Polk reluctantly agreed and Sarah teased him by saying in return for her "sacrifice," he could buy her some new clothes. She tucked into his pocket a list of the things she wanted sent home, a new bonnet and cape and instructions for dresses that were to be made. He left her in Columbia, but his loneliness and longing for her soon convinced him that he never wanted to be without her again, and that was the last winter they spent apart.

His independence in fighting for his own beliefs and his refusal to side with one faction or another, as well as his loyalty to Jackson, increased the President's confidence in him. With so many others jockeying for personal power, Jackson came to depend on Polk even more than he had in the past. He began to look to Polk for strategic help in both the big and little battles of the administration. But the prominence Polk gradually won during Jackson's first term didn't depend on the President's friendship alone. He had to prove his ability in Congress too.

Polk worked hard for a bill to fully extend the benefits of the federal court system to the western states. He fought against plans to distribute the profits from the sale of government lands among all the states, favoring instead a plan to lower land prices and give preference to actual settlers. Battling to reduce federal spending for local improvements, such as a road in Kentucky that he felt was of no national benefit, he attacked Congressmen who "vote for every project so they may get their own projects carried." He said that instead of spending surplus funds on such things, they should be used to lower taxes.

Former President Adams, who after his defeat by Jackson had returned to Washington as a Congressman from Massachusetts, was Polk's chief opponent in a series of stormy debates that went on for months over reapportioning the seats in the House according to the latest census. It was a big step upward for Polk in December, 1831, when he was made chairman of a committee to draft the reapportionment bill. Nearly every member of Congress would be affected by the changes in voting districts and all the states had a jealous interest in the new ratio, which would be used in the next Presidential election. Polk's task was a complicated one of working out hundreds of different tables of representation until he hit upon what seemed the best formula.

Since no ratio would please everyone, his bill was attacked as soon as he introduced it. He was accused of favoring the western states at the expense of Clay's Kentucky, Calhoun's South Carolina, and all of New England. Adams denounced it as an "iniquity" which he said was "effected by disreputable means," and led a group of the unhappy states in forcing a change. But Polk rallied his supporters, made only a slight compromise, and defeated Adams. When the measure came back from the Senate, there was another fight over it, but Polk held the voting strength of the House firmly in line and the Senate finally had to accept the House version. For him, it was not only a victory but also proof of his ability to prepare an involved measure, present it properly, marshall his forces, and then lead it through the tricky parliamentary maze and the debates to final passage.

It involved generalship that Jackson admired and when the next Congress met, Polk was transferred from Foreign Affairs to the House Ways and Means Committee where his skill could be of more help to the administration. He also endeared himself to Jackson by keeping his head in another Congressional controversy when he was deliberately insulted and challenged to a duel by a man he had proved a liar. Although Jackson was a veteran of many duels himself, he praised Polk for ignoring the challenge and avoiding an affair which would have heaped scandal upon the administration.

Polk later defended his old friend Sam Houston when Representative William Stanberry of Ohio accused Houston of fraud in connection with supplying rations to the Indians. Houston himself came to Washington to answer the charges and was so infuriated he bounded to the floor of the House and threatened to beat Stanberry. Polk caught Houston before he could carry out the threat and led him outside to cool off, but a few days later Houston and Stanberry happened to meet on the street and Houston beat the Ohioan with a hickory cane.

Stanberry lodged a complaint with the House and demanded that Houston be arrested and tried for contempt. Polk fought the motion on the grounds that the incident hadn't happened in Congress and that the case would set a dangerous precedent for invasion of liberty, but the shocked members ordered Houston taken into custody and held for trial. Polk defended him before the House, charging that the right to trial by jury was being violated, and after hearings that dragged on for several weeks, finally managed to get him off with the lightest reprimand possible.

He helped prepare and carry on the administration's battle against high tariffs. But it was the part Polk played in Jackson's fight against the bank that really established his leadership in the House. The bank conflict had been smouldering ever since Jackson became President, but it didn't explode until he was about to seek a second term. It was a fight Polk could enter wholeheartedly since he had always been against banking monopoly, paper money, and what he considered an evil combine of government and finance against farmers, workingmen and small business.

The all-powerful Bank of the United States, chartered by Congress, was controlled by its private stockholders as a profit-making enterprise which had the use of the country's money, deposited in its vaults without interest. It was headed by the brilliant and arrogant Philadelphia financier, Nicholas Biddle, who openly boasted that he had for years exercised "more personal authority than any President." This bank had the power to open branches anywhere, to rule the nation's credit and exchange transactions, and to issue bank notes freely. It paid the government a bonus in exchange for its privileges and agreed to handle federal funds without charge. Holding a life and death command over state banks, it could create periods of inflation or depression to influence the voters.

Although the bank's charter wouldn't expire until 1836, the bankers who were supporting Clay for the Presidency against Jackson wanted a recharter bill introduced at once so that if Jackson vetoed the bill, it could be made the main issue of the election battle. Clay was sure that the nation's voters would back the bank and kill Jackson's hope of a second term. In January, 1832, Biddle sent a request for a new charter to Congress. Many of Jackson's own supporters opposed the President's stand against the bank. Committees of both the House and Senate quickly reported in favor of granting the new charter.

Polk joined those who were determined to fight the charter by every possible means. He demanded a searching investigation of the bank's conduct. He accused the bankers of trying to push the charter through without giving the House a chance to consider it fully and said they wouldn't be fighting the request for an investigation unless they had some reason to fear it. The only inference the public could draw from "such shrinking from scrutiny," he declared, was that there was "something rotten in the state of Denmark."

Worried that such charges would turn voters against them, the bank group reluctantly agreed to let a House committee go to Philadelphia to investigate. It wasn't a real investigation since the committee was blocked at every turn by the bank's officials. Nevertheless the investigators uncovered enough to charge that the bank had violated its charter and the report aroused great excitement throughout the country. When Polk prepared copies of it and spread it as widely as possible, his political enemies in Tennessee organized mass meetings to denounce him. They managed to get a grand jury in his own county to pass resolutions favoring the charter and they circulated petitions demanding his recall from Congress. Meanwhile, the strong bank majority in both houses pushed through the recharter bill and it reached the White House on July 4.

"The bank is trying to kill me," Jackson told Van Buren, "but I will kill it!" Against the wishes of every member of his cabinet except Attorney General Roger Taney, the President vetoed the bank charter bill on July 10, attacking the bank's "exclusive privileges to make the rich richer and the potent more powerful." Along with his veto was the opinion by Taney that the bank was unconstitutional. Jackson had put the question before the people to seek their mandate to carry on the fight.

Congress adjourned and Polk went home with the knowledge that if Jackson won his mandate the President would rely on him to lead the battle in the House. The bank poured more money into Clay's campaign than had ever before been spent on a Presidential election. Biddle claimed to be delighted with the veto and predicted that the voters would punish Jackson for it. He said that the bank would "go on in its general business just as if no such event . . . had ever happened."

During that summer of political fury, with the bank trying to discredit him as well as Jackson, Polk also faced tragic family problems. His brother, Franklin, had died an alcoholic in January, 1831, and four months later another brother, Marshall, had died. Marshall, who had settled in North Carolina to practice law, left a young widow, two small children, and heavy debts. Before Polk had time to recover from that double sadness, death came to a third brother, John, who had been a bachelor farmer. Polk took over the responsibility for straightening out the three estates and the care of Marshall's widow and children.

He set up a new law partnership in Columbia mainly to handle the tangled family land and estate transactions, and also gave some of his time to having the land cleared for a new cotton plantation he was starting in the southwestern part of the state. He and Sarah, with no children of their own, turned their affection to his younger brothers, and he took a warm-hearted interest in all the young nephews and nieces of her family as well as his. He saw to it that his sixteen-year-old brother, Bill, was sent to a school in North Carolina to prepare him for entrance to the university, and made a close pal of the last of his brothers still living at home, fourteen-year-old Sam.

In November, when the dust of the election battle settled, Jackson had won his mandate from the people by being elected to a second term as President. Clay and his supporters, who had begun to call themselves Whigs, were stunned by Jackson's overwhelming victory. He had won 219 electoral votes and Clay only 40, and would carry Van Buren into office as his Vice President to replace Calhoun. But Jackson's veto had not yet killed the bank. It still had three years to go under the old charter and the bankers might yet raise enough votes in Congress to override the veto. Biddle and the bank were making a fight for life and Polk rushed back to Washington at Jackson's summons to become the President's unofficial spokesman in the House.

He and Jackson planned their strategy shrewdly. Under the charter, the Secretary of the Treasury could remove the federal deposits from the bank for good cause. Without the nation's money in its vaults, the bank would be out of business. But both Congress and the public would have to be convinced such a drastic act was justified. What was needed first was real evidence against the bank, much more than the token inquiry had produced. "An investigation kills it and its supporters *dead,*" Jackson wrote in a confidential note to Polk two weeks after Congress went into session. "Let this be had—call upon the Secretary of the Treasury who must agree with me that an investigation by Congress is absolutely necessary."

For a month, the Ways and Means Committee met six days a week to hear witnesses and Polk did most of the questioning. Finally, with only a few days left in the session, the pro-bank majority issued a report that the nation's deposits might be continued safely at the bank, as Polk had expected. But he submitted a lengthy minority report, including 134 pages of evidence and supporting testimony, which provided plenty of ammunition for questioning the bank's dealings. In it, he revealed that the bank had so extended its loans it was forced to borrow from a group of British financiers to pay debts of the United States. He went on to show that the bank had tried to postpone government payments and he charged that its manipulations had risked the nation's financial security. Polk declared that the facts would "justify the executive in taking any steps against the bank authorized by the charter" no matter what the opinion of Congress might be.

But there was no time to print the committee reports before they were debated on the last day of the session. Although Polk pleaded with Congress not to "whitewash" the bank without studying all the facts, the members upheld the majority report favoring the bank and then adjourned.

Jackson was inaugurated for his second term and Polk went back to Tennessee to fight to hold his seat in Congress. The bank threw its money and power behind his opponents in the Congressional race. He was accused of undermining credit in the western states and his district was flooded with special editions of a Washington newspaper which gave a false account on his arguments on the bank question. There were two opponents in the election contest against him and three political factions out to defeat him. Cave Johnson, who had entered Congress as a fellow Representative from Tennessee in 1829 and had become one of Polk's closest friends, warned him that "the bank people, with their cunning and money and double-headed game" were determined to see to it that he never returned to Washington. But Polk exposed the tricks being used against him and turned them to his own advantage by showing how much the bankers feared him. He repeated the charges he had made, detailed the facts he had uncovered to support them, and when the contest was over, he had won by twice as many votes as both opponents combined.

One of the public appearances he made during the campaign was at a camp meeting which drew a large crowd to Columbia to hear John B. McFerrin, a forceful young preacher who was to become a Methodist bishop of Tennessee. Though Polk went to the meeting mainly to shake hands with the voters, McFerrin's sermon moved him so deeply it was a religious experience he remembered all his life. Although he was a man of strong faith and a regular church-goer, he had never joined a church. His emotions were so lifted by McFerrin's preaching that he felt like stepping forward with the others that day to be converted. He held back, but years later, when he was dying, he recalled that camp meeting and what had seemed the clear truth of McFerrin's words.

In Washington, meanwhile, Polk's minority report on the bank had encouraged Jackson to make a dramatic move. The President felt that its evidence, along with other developments, made his position strong enough to take the federal deposits from Biddle's control. When Treasury Secretary McLane refused, Jackson twice shifted his cabinet around. For a time, he considered making Polk his Secretary of the Treasury, but decided he needed him more in the House. After firing another Secretary, he finally moved Attorney General Taney to the Treasury post. In September, Jackson announced that all new federal deposits would be made in state banks and that government funds gradually would be removed from the vaults of Biddle's national bank.

By the time Polk reached the capital for the session of Congress that began in December, 1833, Biddle had decided that the only way to save his bank was to cause so much business distress that people would panic and demand that the government restore the deposits and grant the charter. He reduced loans so sharply that businessmen were hard-pressed for funds and then denounced Jackson's "high-handed act" as the cause of the tight-money situation. "Nothing but the evidence of suffering," Biddle wrote an associate, "will produce any effect in Congress."

With a Whig coalition in control of the Senate, Jackson had to rely entirely on the House and Polk was lifted from the bottom of the Ways and Means Committee to be made its chairman and unofficial floor leader for the administration. Jackson's message to Congress on the removal of the deposits was accompanied by a report from

Treasury Secretary Taney. Polk tried to have it referred directly to the committee he headed, but the bank men managed to put it before the whole House.

The House galleries were crowded on the last day of December as Polk began the most important speech he had ever made, one in which all of official Washington and most of the nation was vitally interested. Calling the bank a "great irresponsible rival power of the Government," he said the question was "whether we shall have the republic without the bank or the bank without the republic." He predicted that if the power and monopoly of the bank continued it would become "the veriest despot that ever ruled any land—a despotism of money without responsibility" that would "control your election of the President, of your Senators, and of your Representatives . . . whom it could bend to its own purposes."

Charging the bankers with trying to "flood the country with inflammatory speeches" so as to panic the people, Polk carefully took apart each of the major arguments, one by one, and then presented such a thorough and detailed list of documented facts against the bank's policies and management that its defenders spent most of the following two months trying to answer him. His speech, published in pamphlet form, became a text for Jacksonian newspapers and orators. Jackson himself bought five hundred copies to distribute to important leaders all over the country. At mass meetings from Philadelphia to New Orleans, Polk was toasted as the new hero of democracy.

But the bank men, of course, were far less complimentary. The Biddle-controlled *New York Courier & Enquirer* called his speech "the most alarming made to Congress for some years past" and warned the Whigs not to underestimate Polk's "daily evidence of industry and research," declaring that he had become "more the organ of the administration than any other individual on the floor of the House of Representatives." Former President Adams, calling him "the leader of the administration," noted in his diary that Polk had none of the fancy airs of fine oratory, "no gracefullness of delivery, no elegance of language, no felicitious impromptus," but grudgingly admitted that his old enemy showed great "confidence, fluency and labor."

Finally, more than two months after it had been sent to the House, Polk won his fight to have the question of the President's removal of the bank deposits referred to his committee. He made a 141-page report, supporting Jackson and elaborating on his speech to document the charges that Biddle and the bankers deliberately had tried to create a financial panic to bring pressure on Congress. With that pressure growing, Polk defended his committee report through another month of furious debate. In a series of bitter floor fights, he carried the resolution against a new bank charter, another against restoring the deposits, a third to continue deposits in state banks, and then put through a bill for a full and sweeping investigation.

Biddle defied Congress and stubbornly refused to cooperate with the investigators or to let them examine the bank's books. Polk was kept informed of the committee's frustrations in Philadelphia by his former Chapel Hill classmate, John Mason, then a Representative from Virginia and a member of the investigating group. Demands were made to bring Biddle before the House and cite him for contempt, but by then the war against the bank had been won on every count and Jackson had been vindicated. The bank was thoroughly discredited and except for the formalities of winding up its affairs, it was dead. "Polk, for the hard service done in the cause," said President Jackson, "deserves a medal from the American people."

Polk wasn't about to rest on his laurels, however, for he had another battle to wage that was equally important to him personally in terms of his future. All during the height of the bank controversy, with the active help of his friend Cave Johnson and the support of the President, he had been seeking election as Speaker of the House. Before the contest was over, it would split the Jackson forces completely, in both Tennessee and in the nation, and for a time even threaten Martin Van Buren's chances of becoming the next President.

Chapter Eight

PRESIDENT JACKSON was so sure James Polk would be chosen Speaker of the House on June 2, 1834, that he planned an informal little party at the White House for Polk and a few other close friends. The refreshments were ready and when word was received that the balloting had begun at the Capitol, Jackson sent his carriage down Pennsylvania Avenue to pick up the guests as soon as Polk's election by the members of Congress was confirmed. But the coachman returned without Polk and with news that put Jackson in a "miserable bad humor" for days. Polk hadn't been chosen. He had been defeated for the Speakership by his fellow Tennesseean, John Bell.

Up until then, Bell generally had been considered a loyal Jacksonian. It wasn't publicly known that he was deeply in debt to Biddle and the bank or that he had made good friends among the Whigs to further his own ambitions. Bell had gathered behind him the support of various anti-Jackson factions in Congress, as well as some Jackson men who thought Polk and the President had gone too far in their fight against the bank. Although Polk was a dozen votes ahead of him on the first ballot, the Speakership was Bell's by the time the tenth count was taken. Branded a traitor to the cause by Jackson as well as by Polk, Bell soon sided more openly with those who had elected him Speaker. Bell and Polk became uncompromising enemies, each determined to overthrow the political power of the other in Tennessee, with results that were to have national significance.

Greatly disappointed by his loss of the Speakership and exhausted by the long Congressional fight over the bank, Polk became ill and was forced to stay in bed during most of the remaining few weeks of the session. By the time Congress adjourned and he returned to Columbia, he discovered Bell was already hard at work organizing an alliance against him. Polk hit back at once and the split in Tennessee politics widened. One of Polk's problems was that Bell's group managed to influence most of the state's newspapers which were in control of owners favorable to banking interests, so he eventually started a Nashville paper of his own.

Jackson meanwhile came out flatly for a hard money policy, saying there was no need for banks or for paper bank notes to replace honest coins of the realm, a theory that fitted well with Polk's old principles. But Sarah became a little annoyed when her husband insisted on carrying the principles into practice by paying hard cash for everything. She complained that filling her purse with coins made it too heavy to carry around. It was a particular bother to her when they were traveling and she had to take along a supply of coins to meet expenses. On one trip, she had to pull all their clothes out of the trunk to find a bag of coins so he would have money to pay a man.

"Don't you see how troublesome it is to carry around gold and silver?" she asked. "This is enough to show you how useful banks are."

He laughed and answered, "Sarah, you've turned your politics."

His cotton plantation in western Tennessee hadn't been doing too well and, still searching for new frontiers, he bought some recently opened Indian lands in Mississippi in the fall of 1834 and made arrangements for starting another plantation there. For a while, he owned it in partnership with one of his brothers-in-law, but later bought out his share to become sole owner.

The trip back to Washington that fall was a happy family adventure. His youngest brother, Sam, was about to enter Yale, along with two of his nephews and another young man from Columbia, and he and Sarah escorted them to New Haven. They had their first exciting ride on the new railroad cars that ran from Frederick, Maryland, to Baltimore. In Philadelphia and again in New York, he took his young companions sight-seeing while Sarah went on a shopping spree in the stores. The Polks sailed from New York up the Long Island Sound to New Haven and left the boys there to go on to Washington, loaded down with things they had bought on the way, including an armful of books for winter reading that ranged from *Don Quixote* to Washingon Irving's *Sketch Book*.

Polk found no pleasure, however, in the news awaiting him that Bell and his group in Tennessee were strongly supporting the state's popular Senator and former judge, Hugh White, as a candidate for President in 1836. White, who had been Polk's close friend and Jackson's ally, was now determined to challenge Jackson's power by working against Van Buren for the Presidency. With Bell's help and the backing of the bankers, the Whigs might destroy the Jacksonians in their own state or even in other states with other candidates.

The movement grew alarmingly all through the winter and into the spring of 1835. With the Presidential contest only a year away, Polk faced his own battle for reelection to Congress. Sentiment for White was so strong in Tennessee that most of the state's leading Democrats refused to attend the party's national convention at Baltimore in May that nominated Van Buren. Polk's own district was filled with Bell and White supporters and Bell personally promised banker Biddle that Polk would be defeated at the polls.

Polk fought not only for his own place in the House, but to try to save Tennessee for the Jacksonians and Van Buren. He began his campaign while the opposition was still trying to decide on a Congressional candidate to run against him.

It was a campaign that helped him polish the speaking style that made him one of the most popular public speakers the state had ever known. Polk had never been a fiery arm-waving orator. He much preferred appeals to logic and reason. His personality wasn't that of the typical politician. Although he was warmly friendly in his relationships with those close to him, he was a quiet man, reserved and serious-minded, methodical and deliberate in his manner and not one to capture the public with any electric spark of personal charm.

But he had schooled himself in the political art of making friends wherever he went and he had a phenomenal memory. It was said that Polk never forgot the name of any man whose hand he shook and years later could recall the exact circumstances of their meeting. As he neared forty, he was an impressive-looking individual, short but solidly built, with an erect square-shouldered bearing and a bristling air of energy. There was a pioneer ruggedness about his high-cheekboned face beneath the unruly black hair that he brushed straight back from his broad forehead. His dark skin had a taut and weathered look, his nose was long and prominent, his chin square and he had large and intense steel-gray eyes.

It was a face he used expressively, with grins, grimaces, sly glances, a wry twisting of his mouth, to drive home the sallies of wit and sarcasm that brought laughter and shouts of delight from his listeners. When he took to the stump to address the backwoods crowds, he threw off some of the natural dignity that was his in Washington. He would mimic his opponents, both in voice and expression, but still without ever making himself a clown.

He probably had little sleep as he rode to every remote village of his district throughout that long summer, driving himself without rest until his health broke down. In the last few days before election, he was forced to stay home in bed. Polk won in his own district, but in the rest of Tennessee the results were a disaster for the Jacksonians. The Bell-White combine won nearly every important contest in the state. Although the Democrats had carried their elections in the rest of the nation, Tennessee had deserted Jackson. The next year, in the Presidential race, White would capture the electoral votes of Tennessee against Van Buren. Even though Georgia was to be the only other state in which White won, Jackson's opponents had taken the power away from him in what had been his stronghold.

Seriously ill for a time, Polk went to Beaver Dam Springs for a complete rest where he could shut himself off from all the problems and worries of politics. His recovery was slow and when he finally had to return to Columbia, he was still in poor health. Planning for the trip to Washington, he heard from friends that some of Van Buren's men, considering Tennessee already lost in the Presidential election that was ahead, thought that the next Speaker of the House should be chosen from some other state. But others felt that because of his fight for Van Buren against Bell and White, Polk should have the party's solid backing.

In Washington, when the party leaders gathered in caucus before Congress met, Polk finally won their full endorsement. On December 7, 1835, the House gave him 132 votes to 84 for Bell, and Polk replaced him as Speaker. He was escorted to the chair and made a brief speech of thanks. When the news reached Tennessee, the Jacksonians staged cheering celebrations. In many towns, candles lighted the windows of homes and people paraded the streets, some of them firing guns into the air in jubilation over his victory and Bell's defeat, while crowds shouted, "Polk and Van Buren!"

But Mr. Speaker Polk faced a rebellious Congress divided by sectional feuds, party battles and violent personal hatreds. This tested not only his ability to think clearly and act firmly, but also his temper and his tact, his cool-headed restraint despite a constant barrage of insults and even threats to beat him or to shoot him. Polk greatly expanded the authority of the office and made many parliamentary rulings that were to guide future Speakers. With the two-party system just beginning to take definite form, he was the first Speaker frankly recognized as a party leader. He devoted much of his time to planning and carrying out the strategy that would put the Democratic program through the House.

His position gave him enormous influence as well as heavy responsibility in appointing the committees, deciding the order of business, and controlling the flow of debate. His private office, off to one side of the House chamber, was always filled with the committee chairmen and party leaders who came to consult him and he had a personal porter to help limit the job seekers, tourists and others who sought favors or just wanted to say they had shaken his hand.

In addition to committee meetings in the mornings and House sessions that usually began right after lunch and lasted until late in the afternoon, Polk had a number of administrative duties, such as managing the clerk and doorkeeper and their staffs and overseeing the remodeling of the House chamber. Bad acoustics remained a problem, with members still complaining they couldn't be heard properly, and the chairs had just been shifted back to their original positions. Polk occupied a new Speaker's desk, high above the floor, with a crimson canopy above it. But there was little formality about the sessions themselves, with members moving around as they pleased and busily talking to each other while the debates went on.

Being leader of the party in power, Polk made sure the Democrats had a heavy majority on all the important committees. However, he also made some appointments that annoyed the die-hards in his own party and surprised his enemies. Recognizing the special talents of old John Quincy Adams, he named him chairman of the Committee of Manufactures. Polk chose another Whig to head the Committee on Roads and appointed a third to the important Foreign Affairs Committee. He surprised everybody by making his arch-enemy, former Speaker John Bell, chairman of the Committee on Indian Affairs. But if he hoped to soften up the fury of his opponents, he was quickly disappointed. Under Bell's leadership they began an immediate and unrelenting campaign to harass him in every possible way and to subject him to an ordeal of abuse more determined than any Speaker had ever met.

Assisting Bell were Representatives Wise and Peyton

who let hardly any action of Polk's pass without an annoying interruption. They jumped to their feet to question points of order, to defy parliamentary rulings, to make wordy appeals from his decisions, and to heap personal insults upon him. They hoped, by means of their daily war of nerves, to wear out Polk's patience so he would lose his temper and create a scene, to trap him in some way that would drive him from the Speaker's chair, or at least to cause so much continuing turmoil that people would be convinced he was unable to maintain order in the House.

Planning their attacks each night at the boarding house where they all lived, they seized upon every petty excuse to trouble him or to call him names. They tried to hurt him even more by making something of a public sport of baiting the Speaker, letting it be known in advance in the capital's bars and hotels whenever they had some special maneuver planned so that crowds would pack the visitors' galleries the next day in the hope of watching Polk squirm. But Polk ignored their insults, kept both his temper and his good judgment, and wouldn't be taunted into making decisions that went against the rules of the House.

He let them wear themselves out by deliberately refusing to take notice of their insults. On the few occasions that he did answer them, it was with quiet dignity, without passion, and simply to recite the facts involved in the situation. By his obvious fairness in not halting their tirades, he won the support of many Whigs as well as Democrats and soon was able to unite the House in voting down his opponents, so that members came to look upon Wise and Peyton as nuisances. The same strategy often kept Bell from getting the floor to make speeches denouncing Polk.

His tormentors, infuriated by his calm, then planned to drag Polk into a duel. News of the plot was common gossip as far away as Tennessee and Polk's brother-in-law, James Walker, warned him of it in a letter from home and reminded him that "moral courage is the highest virtue." Wise found an excuse one day when Polk had been forced to call him to order a number of times. After the session was over, Wise met Polk at the House door, swore at him, called him the vilest of names, and openly challenged him to a duel. The Washington newspapers supporting Bell's group tried to force Polk to take up the challenge by calling him a coward. When he still ignored the whole thing, Peyton circulated false reports of the affair in Tennessee newspapers, quoting Jackson as saying if Polk "meant to submit to such indignities he had better resign and go home."

The President was furious when he learned of the lies Peyton had put in his mouth. He promptly announced that he "highly approved" Polk's conduct and good judgment. "In treating such blackguardism with contempt," Jackson said that Polk had "pursued the course that was most consistent with the dignity of the House and just self-respect." But the failure of the plot didn't halt the attacks against Polk and Bell himself managed to get the floor of the House later to accuse the Speaker of being as much a menial in the hire of the administration as one of Jackson's slaves.

Polk's problems didn't come from the Bell camp alone. With so many controversial issues before the House, there was hardly any ruling he could make that didn't stir up outraged protest by one group or another. Although those who wanted to abolish slavery were then still a small and unpopular minority in the north as well as in the south, the question became part of many debates. Polk tried to take a moderate stand, to preserve national unity, and put an end to what he considered the "dangerously inflammable discussions" by agitators on both sides. With Van Buren's election still to come, the Democrats wanted to avoid the discussion of any issue that might alienate northern voters.

Texas was another of the subjects Polk tried to keep out of debate, even though he felt strongly about it himself. Sam Houston had gone there several years before with the aim of eventually annexing the Mexican province to the United States, a move which Jackson encouraged, and Polk's own family had been involved in the Texan war for independence. Two of his cousins had nearly lost their lives in it, and his great-uncle, Thomas Hardeman, wrote him in March, 1836, to give Polk a first-hand account of the massacre of the defenders of the Alamo. "We are looking to the United States to acknowledge our independence and give us all the assistance they can," the letter said. "James, you have an active tongue. Why not use it for Texas, as all true Americans should do under existing circumstances?"

In the years ahead, Polk was to "use his tongue" most actively in behalf of Texas' annexation, but he was forced to hold it then because Van Buren decided, and Jackson agreed, that it was a poor time to argue the question. Some northerners, led in the House by Adams, considered the move to add Texas to the United States merely part of a southern conspiracy to extend slavery and Polk had many sharp clashes with Adams. On one occasion, the former President tried to force the matter to debate during a roll-call of the members present. The House was thrown into complete disorder, with Congressmen angrily shouting at each other, until Polk firmly took control and declared that Adams was violating the parliamentary rules. But despite their enmity, Polk treated Adams with consideration, even though he didn't like him, and in a later session he approved a measure Adams proposed to outlaw dueling in the District of Columbia.

Heavily burdened as he was by his duties and troubles in Congress, Polk nevertheless conducted a tireless campaign by mail to rouse the Democrats back home in Tennessee to keep up their political fight against the growing strength of the Whigs. From Washington, he sent a flood of letters to his friends, urging them to do battle, advising them on details of campaign strategy, supplying them with pamphlets, newspaper articles and copies of speeches.

As soon as the Congressional session adjourned in July, 1836, he went to Tennessee and put all his energy into the speech-making and rallies for Van Buren. Although the fight was unsuccessful, in that the Democrats lost Tennessee while Van Buren was winning the votes of the rest of the nation, Polk began to emerge as the party's leader in the state. In all the following election campaigns during his years as Speaker, he rushed home as soon as each session closed to make speeches up and down the state, to revitalize the party, and gradually became its acknowledged chieftain.

Warned by his friend Cave Johnson that Wise and Peyton planned still another attempt to draw him into a duel, Polk took the chair as Speaker when Congress met in December, 1836, for the last session under President Jackson's administration. He faced not only the continuing harassment by his personal enemies, but also an effort by the Whigs to discredit the outgoing President. Investigating committees tried to implicate Jackson in all sorts of sinister plots and one witness dramatically charged that Peyton had aimed a pistol and threatened his life at a committee hearing. But the committees, under Polk's control, returned reports clearing Jackson.

On Inauguration Day in March, when Van Buren took over the Presidency, Jackson was at the height of his popularity, still the adored hero of the people, and Polk was chosen to take charge of his homeward journey, to shield the retiring chief executive as much as possible from the outpouring mobs who hailed him all along the route back to Tennessee. It was an exhausting and nerve-wracking experience for Polk, trying to lead the aging Jackson safely through the wildly cheering crowds, the jostling and confusion at every step. Polk and Sarah narrowly escaped injury themselves in a railroad accident shortly after leaving the capital. He managed to get the Jackson party aboard a steamboat for the trip down the Ohio River, marked by riotous receptions in the towns along the way, and a great celebration at Cincinnati. Finally, he brought Jackson safely to Nashville and he and Sarah, as tired out as the ex-President, escaped to Murfreesboro for a vacation with her relatives.

But Polk had little chance to enjoy his much-needed rest. There was bad news from all parts of the country. Banks and business houses were failing and, as the whole structure of speculative credit came tumbling down, the nation soon was in the grip of the worst financial panic in its history. The Whigs tried to throw all the blame on the monetary policies of the Democrats and there was a quickly growing demand to restore the old privately controlled Bank of the United States.

The Polks had been planning to go on from Murfreesboro to spend some time with Jackson at the Hermitage, but he abandoned the trip as well as the rest of his vacation and went back to Columbia instead to sound out public opinion in his district. In letters and speeches, he tried to offset the charges against the Democrats and the clamor for reviving the bank. Pointing out that the panic was worldwide, Polk argued that it "could not have been caused by acts of the Government," and said that the real cause was the "mania for speculation in lands, stocks and merchandise . . . and every description of property; in wild and extravagant trading" which he blamed on the use of paper money.

Words, however, were not enough to fight a depression, and President Van Buren called for a special session of Congress to meet the first Monday in September, 1837, to deal with the crisis. The Democrats still had a majority in the House, but conservatives among them were siding with the Whigs, and Polk's re-election as Speaker was in jeopardy. He arrived in Washington a week early and immediately began a hectic round of political talks that finally won him the Speakership again, but only by a scant 13 votes over his old enemy, John Bell. What was equally serious was that the coalition of conservative Democrats and Whigs, voting together, would be able to block many administration measures and give Polk even more trouble in trying to control the House.

During the special session that lasted through mid-October, Polk successfully fought a continuing battle to limit debate solely to the financial problems outlined in Van Buren's message to Congress. Van Buren had proposed an independent government treasury, belonging to the people and isolated from all private banks, but opponents managed to have the measure tabled because it called for using only coins instead of paper money. The special session passed emergency measures to pull the government out of threatened bankruptcy, including one to authorize ten million dollars in Treasury notes.

Polk then made a flying trip to Tennessee, riding night and day to reach Columbia in a little more than a week and leaving Sarah behind to catch up with him. He went to work to bolster the Democratic party in the state, openly branding Bell and his group Whigs rather than Democrats. Exposing the alliance of the conservatives with the northern Whigs in a way the voters could understand, Polk was honored at a dinner attended by party leaders from all parts of Tennessee. Still with little rest, driving himself so his health suffered, he raced back to Washington with Sarah for the start of the regular December Congress.

Van Buren's independent treasury bill topped the agenda, but despite all of Polk's planning and his efforts to push it through, the measure failed to pass in that session as it would in the next. But the fight over it in the spring of 1838 added to the list of Polk's enemies in the House.

Feelings became so violent that Polk's personal safety was threatened. Shocking proof of that violence came in February when a Whig Representative from Kentucky, William Graves, challenged a Democrat from Maine, Jonathan Cilley, to a duel. Wise, who acted as Graves' second, was accused of deliberately provoking the encounter, just as he had tried to lure Polk into a duel. The two Congressmen met on a field at Bladensburg, Maryland, with rifles as their weapons, and at a distance of eighty yards fired three rounds before Graves shot Cilley dead.

Three months later, a new Democratic Congressman from Tennessee, Hopkins Turney, and Bell got into a hand-to-hand fight on the floor of the House. Turney charged in a debate that Bell had deserted both his principles and his party for personal gain. Bell, sitting just behind him, lost his temper and shouted that Polk had put Turney up to making the charge because Polk was afraid to fight him in a duel. Turney called him a liar and Bell took a swing at him. The two fell upon each other to fight it out and Polk, who had not been presiding at the moment, rushed to the Speaker's chair and finally managed to restore order.

He compelled both men to apologize to the House. Then, to show his fairness, Polk permitted Bell to finish his scathing remarks against him. Wise later tried to stir up a duel between Turney and Bell, but Polk talked Turney out of accepting the challenge. Polk also avoided another plot to involve him in a street brawl with Bell. A letter to Wise from Peyton, who by then had left Congress and moved to New Orleans, suggested Wise should get Bell to "pull Polk's nose on some pretext and get into a fight with him."

When Polk became Speaker, he and Sarah had to get larger living quarters to allow for the increased entertaining expected of him in his new position. Socially, the Polks became part of a very select inner circle. He was ranked by official Washington in the same group with the President, Vice President and cabinet officers. They were frequent guests at the White House, at small dinner parties for visiting dignitaries and other honored notables, and gave their own parties for guests whom the ordinary Congressman wasn't expected to entertain.

They took a suite of rooms at a fashionable Pennsylvania Avenue establishment where there were facilities for additional parlors and dining rooms when their guest list was unusually large. Their old Tennessee friend, Judge Catron, who had become a justice of the Supreme Court, also lived in the same building, along with several other justices, and Mrs. Catron was among Sarah's closest companions. Her other acquaintances were the wives of the capital's most important men and Sarah, thoroughly enjoying her role, made herself extremely popular and well-liked. Many of the wives of Polk's political opponents also counted themselves Sarah's friends.

One of their receptions, to which several hundred people were invited, was rated by the pioneer woman gossip columnist, Anne Royall, as "the genteelest party that has been given this winter by far." But Sarah did put her foot down when it came to attending the nearby horse races and she objected when callers came to discuss political business with Polk on Sunday mornings. She discouraged such visits by walking into the room, dressed to go out, smiling pleasantly, and reminding Polk that it was the Sabbath and time they left for church. He had a luxurious carriage built for them, which the coachmaker called "the most splendid and best furnished ever turned out by me." Lined with claret-colored silk, it had matching curtains, glass windows with Venetian blinds, and gleaming brass lanterns.

Their young niece, Jane Walker, came to Washington to stay with them early in 1838 and they enjoyed having her company. But family trouble and then tragedy soon entered their lives again. Polk's youngest brother, Sam, always his favorite, was suspended from Yale for taking part in a campus demonstration that turned into a riot. Polk had him come to Washington, where he could keep an eye on him, but Sam became ill soon after arriving. He had one illness after another and by early summer the doctors suspected he might be developing tuberculosis. Unable to leave Washington because of his duties in the House, Polk worried constantly over Sam and gave him all the care the best physicians in the capital could provide.

As soon as the session ended in July, he took the family

to New York to consult specialists about Sam's condition. When they held out little hope, Polk took his brother to Philadelphia for more medical examinations, but the doctors there said they could do nothing. He arranged to take Sam home by the most comfortable route and he and Sarah did what they could to keep up the young man's spirits during the sad journey by train, canal boat, steamboat and finally a chartered coach that carried them the last of the way to Columbia.

While Sam's illness grew worse, Polk was forced to wage the political battles expected of him as the state's party chief. So tired he could hardly keep going, he hit the speech-making trail, made the necessary appearances at public gatherings, and carried on the heavy correspondence needed to spark a Democratic revival. There were signs of a turn in the voting strength, a growing chance to reclaim Tennessee for the party, and he told Sarah he couldn't let up for a minute, no matter how he felt, as long as he was able to ride, shake hands and speak to the crowds.

There was also a vital decision he had to make, one on which his future would depend. He had gone about as far as he could go in Congress. As Speaker, he held the highest position the House could offer him, but if the Whigs and conservative Democrats did gain full control, he might lose the Speakership in sessions to come. Meanwhile, friends had started a quiet campaign to win him the possible Vice Presidential nomination in the next national election. Even stronger were the urgings of those who wanted him to run for the governorship of Tennessee. They said he was the only man who could win back the state for the Democrats and that if he did, it would be the best stepping-stone he could give himself to high national office.

Late in August, he was invited to speak at a public dinner attended by a crowd of two thousand people in a grove near Murfreesboro. The stage had been set and when leaders rose to offer a toast calling on Polk to be governor, he replied to the "surprise call to duty" by announcing, as the crowd cheered, that he would be a candidate in 1839. He had decided to risk his political life, to give up a safe seat in Congress from a sure home district, and appeal to the people of a state which had given the Whigs a heavy majority for four years. Polk started an immediate campaign, drawing out crowds to hear him that were bigger than any seen at political rallies in Tennessee for years. All through September and October, he stumped the state, until his voice gave out and his strength almost did. But the response was enthusiastic.

He made a brief visit to his plantation in Mississippi, came back to Tennessee for a final campaign speech and then, with only a week to relax, started out with Sarah for Washington and his last session as Speaker of the House. His brother Sam was still alive, but Polk left Columbia knowing he might never see him again. When he and Sarah reached Washington, there was a letter waiting for them saying another brother, the next youngest, Bill, was in serious trouble.

Back home in Columbia, a man had insulted Bill and he had horsewhipped him in public. The man had threatened to kill him and the two of them had met on the main street to shoot it out. In the exchange, Bill had fatally wounded him. He faced an indictment for murder, but the grand jury finally decided he had acted in self-defense and reduced the charge to assault. Tried on that charge, Bill had been fined and sentenced to six months in prison.

With the added family troubles and his concern for his

own political future weighing upon him, Polk took up his duties as Speaker in a Congress where his enemies were determined to make a final attempt to destroy his reputation and hurt him in the coming Tennessee contest for the governorship. A government scandal in New York gave them the ammunition. The Collector of the Port had been accused of taking huge sums of money and Wise demanded a Congressional investigation. He used the demand to make a vicious attack against Polk's rule of the House, accusing him of having packed earlier investigating committees to hide administration failures. Wise demanded that the House refuse to let Polk appoint the members of the new committee and moved to have them chosen instead by a vote of the whole House. The Virginian had the votes to carry the motion and, although the investigation failed to produce much in the way of results, it was a damaging blow to Polk.

Meanwhile, the letters from home were filled with grief. Sarah had a brief note from his stricken brother, Sam, a pitiful message in which he thanked her for her kindness to him and said she had been "more a mother than a sister" in the tender care she had given him on his trip home and while they were in Columbia. A few days later, another letter came from Polk's mother. Sam had died, the fourth of her sons she had to bury, and a fifth one was in jail.

Even as Congress finally came to a close, to end the fourteen hectic years he had served, Polk was subjected to a final insult. Some of his opponents tried to get the House to refuse him the customary vote of thanks for the "able, impartial and dignified manner" in which he had presided as Speaker.

But Congress overwhelmingly refused to go along with it. It passed the original resolution of thanks by a wide majority. In a brief farewell speech to the members, Polk said he valued their vote even more than he ordinarily might have because the circumstances had made it more than a routine gesture. He did not exaggerate when he said, "It has been made my duty to decide more questions of parliamentary law and order, many of them of a complex and difficult character . . . than had been decided by all my predecessors from the formation of this government."

He had no need to add what the members already knew, that no other Speaker ever had faced more torment and personal abuse from a small group of determined enemies. Polk had kept his temper and his sense of judgment and escaped all their plots, and had served the office with ability and dignity that finally won him more admiration than hate. He and Sarah both felt a sadness in leaving Washington. There were those who said he was sacrificing his career in national politics for the almost hopeless task of reclaiming Tennessee for his party. But he already had his ambition set beyond the governorship on a much higher goal that he hoped would bring him back to Washington some day.

Chapter Nine

BEFORE JAMES POLK'S campaign against Governor Newton Cannon was over, feelings were so aroused there were violent street fights in many Tennessee villages. But Polk's own debates with Cannon produced more laughter than violence and it was his wit as much as his serious arguments that won the voters. He put his sense of humor to work to confound the enemies who had tried to picture him as a "man who never smiled."

Polk started his campaign to reclaim Tennessee for the Democrats on a serious note with a 28-page statement of his principles in which he defended his record in Congress and called for a reform of the state's banking laws. He summed up the history of the long struggle between those he accused of distrusting the will of the people and those who believed government should carry popular will into effect. Saying it should be a "matter of thrilling interest to every patriotic man" to extend popular education to "the great mass of the community," he pointed to his long fight to secure funds for a greater public school system and declared, "No people who are not enlightened can long remain free." He had thousands of copies printed for distribution throughout the state, busily held conferences to decide on the party's candidates for lesser offices, and began his active campaign at Murfreesboro in April.

Cannon was in the audience and when Polk invited him to debate, the governor said he hadn't come prepared to speak but might make a reply. Polk spoke for two and a half hours and Cannon's "reply" lasted another hour and a half before Polk took the platform again for a rebuttal. Cannon was a slow and dull speaker who had been a loyal Democrat and still wasn't quite sure how far he wanted to go in supporting the Whigs. Polk ridiculed Cannon and gave the crowd a rousing good show. He mimicked Henry Clay, puffed out his cheeks and imitated the portly strut of Daniel Webster, and made hilarious fun of other Whig leaders.

Later the same week, Polk had another crowd laughing with him and at Cannon throughout a four-hour debate. His old enemy Bell, who was in that audience, jumped to the platform in a "rage of passion" and launched into an angry tirade that lasted until dark. But Bell so lost his temper that the listeners turned against him and the people cheered when Polk met his fury with calm and good-humored answers. "The day was ours and our opponents knew it," he wrote Sarah that night. "Bell did more for us than I and all our friends could have done."

Busy at home mailing out campaign literature, handling his correspondence and arranging Polk's speaking schedule, Sarah was much concerned that he was driving himself too hard. In the affectionate letters they exchanged, she pleaded with him to take care of himself, and when he wasn't able to write for a few days, she became deeply worried. "I am anxious to hear from you," she said in one of her notes, "not political prospects only, but your *health*."

Cannon soon realized he was no match for Polk in their direct encounters and gave up the debates. He confined himself mostly to making statements to the press while he let other Whig speakers confront Polk in public. But for Polk, the campaign had just started. He spoke every day and traveled into even the smallest mountain villages. Groups sometimes would meet him along the road and Polk would swing down from his horse and make a speech to them right there. In two months, he rode more than 1,300 miles through thirty-seven counties, wore out his own horse and had to leave it behind and ride hired ones, and made hundreds of impromptu talks as well as more than forty major speeches.

The results were so close the outcome of the election was in doubt for nearly a week before it was decided that Polk had become governor of Tennessee by a slim majority of less than 2,500 votes. Democrats had greatly increased their voting strength throughout the state and had captured the legislature and doubled the number of their Representatives in Congress. Although Bell had managed to keep his own Congressional seat, he wrote to a friend, "I am done, *done* as a public man." Clay, already in fear that William Henry Harrison might win the Whig Presidential nomination away from him in 1840, called Polk's victory "a most disastrous event, which, I fear, is likely to exercise great, if not fatal, influence far beyond the limits of Tennessee."

Jackson, of course, was overjoyed and congratulations also came to Polk from members of Van Buren's cabinet and from Democratic Congressmen throughout the country. Great victory celebrations were held in Tennessee, with the firing of cannon and torchlight parades. Sam Houston, then visiting the state as a hero of Texan independence, addressed a dinner at Murfreesboro, where toasts were offered to Washington, Jefferson, and Polk.

Sarah and he celebrated by joining Jackson and other leading Democrats and their families at Tyree Springs, a resort near Nashville, for a week's rest and recreation. The guests made a pact to forbid all talk of politics and enjoyed the refreshing spring waters and the sunny days. For fun, they held a mock court every morning after breakfast under the elms in the yard. Felix Grundy, then Van Buren's Attorney General and about to resign from the cabinet to return to the Senate, was the "Chief Justice" and Jackson was his "Associate Justice." The prominent guests were brought up before the make-believe court on all sorts of amusing charges, such as failure to bow properly to a passing young lady, and their "fines" were used to buy fruits and sweets for the men and flowers for their wives.

People from all parts of the state crowded into Nashville for Polk's inauguration as governor on October 14, 1839. The two houses of the legislature marched in procession from their courthouse chambers to the Presbyterian church where the ceremonies were held, after a prayer by a Baptist minister and a brief speech by retiring Governor Cannon. A seat of honor had been reserved for Jackson and the aging ex-President beamed with obvious delight as Polk attacked the Whigs, the banks, and high tariffs in an inaugural address in which he declared once again that the "ultimate and supreme authority rests in the People."

Since the state provided no executive mansion, the Polks rented a large brick house, with a pleasant garden and separate kitchen and stables, on one of Nashville's better streets for $500 a year. Polk's salary as governor was only $2,000 and, like his meager salary during all the years he was in Congress, it didn't begin to meet his expenses. Although he was wealthy in terms of property, he was financially hard-pressed for immediate funds and was carrying heavy family debts. His plantation was just beginning to bring an income that would help him meet his obligations, but hard times had made land sales difficult and he had poured much of his money into party campaigns, newspapers, pamphlets, and other efforts in the Democratic cause. In addition, he had been forced to neglect his own business because of his political activities. While he was by no means a poor man, he became more cautious about spending, especially for entertaining.

However, Sarah was active in the city's social life and gradually encouraged him, for his own sake, since she felt he was working too hard, to join her in attending various affairs. Sometimes he would beg off on the plea that he couldn't afford "to lose half a day just to go out and dine." On several occasions, she went to functions without him, and after that he usually accompanied her. Independent as always in her social contacts, she formed many new friendships among the Whig families who dominated Nashville society. Polk's own attitude became more tolerant, agreeing with Sarah that they shouldn't let the opposing political views of their friends anger them since "every man has the right to his own opinion, wrong though he may be."

Without any secretarial help, he found the routine work of the governorship a drudgery that involved the signing of countless official papers, pardons, and commissions. Polk insisted on giving careful consideration even to the smallest matters, especially when they involved what might be regarded as a favor to a friend or relative, and was meticulously honest in carrying out his executive business to the letter of the law. He gave his party strong legislative leadership in planning measures and organizing the strategy to carry them through, although his own interest was more in national than in state affairs.

Two days after he became governor, his friends introduced a resolution in the state senate proposing that Tennessee nominate him as its candidate for Vice President. Within a week, the resolution was put through both houses. Democratic newspapers in the state joined in suggesting Polk as Van Buren's running mate on the party's next national ticket. Several New England papers also gave their approval and the boom began to catch on. In Washington, his friends Cave Johnson and Aaron Brown were working hard to get him the nomination.

Although Polk remained in the background, the bid was carefully planned. His election victory in Tennessee had put him in high standing with the party nationally. His friends pointed out that he could help Van Buren take southern votes from Henry Clay, who was expected to be nominated by the Whigs for President. Democratic leaders in North Carolina, Ohio, New York, and Virginia, as well as in New England, were said to be swinging to Polk's support. Ex-President Jackson lent his influence by sending Andrew Donelson, his nephew and personal secretary, to Washington to work with the group seeking the Vice Presidential nomination for Polk. Jackson also sent a letter to Van Buren, urging him to choose Polk as a running mate "whose popularity would strengthen you."

But the prospects which had seemed so bright began to fade. The Whigs, at their national convention in December, dropped Clay and unexpectedly nominated William Henry Harrison for President. Some Democrats felt Polk's strength in the south was no longer as vital. There were other contenders for the Vice Presidential nomination and the incumbent Richard Johnson wanted to run again with Van Buren. Polk finally announced that he was willing to become a candidate, but not on a sectional basis, and that he wouldn't run at all unless he had the backing of the entire party.

Early in March, he made a trip to his plantation in Mississippi, and by the time he returned to Nashville his friends in Washington thought his hope of winning the nomination looked very dim. Polk went on fighting for it right up to the time the Democrats held their national convention at Baltimore in April and named Van Buren as their Presidential candidate. But after long debate, the convention voted not to nominate any candidate for Vice President. The delegates at Baltimore left it up to the Democrats in the various states to decide on their own candidates for Vice President. Whoever won the support of electors in most of the states would have been named to the office if Van Buren had become President.

Despite his disappointment, Polk accepted the decision gracefully and issued a statement that he would abide by it. Whig newspapers in Tennessee were joyful over his failure to win the nomination. One of them, the *Nashville Republican Banner,* predicted "his party will be overthrown and he along with it . . . henceforth, his career will be downwards." Although Polk's friends, including many Jackson men, privately blamed Van Buren for not coming out strongly for Polk, he threw himself into the campaign to help re-elect the Democratic President.

He hadn't given up his personal battle, however, to win the Vice Presidency, if not this time, then four years ahead. Even in failure, Polk had gained new prominence as a Democratic leader. He was still a young man in terms of national office, only forty-four, and he could afford momentary defeat. The important thing was for him to keep his own standing in the party and his control in Tennessee. At a rally in Knoxville on the Fourth of July, he announced that he would be a candidate for re-election as governor in 1841. He then took to the stump for Van Buren and attacked the "humbuggery" of the Whig "hard cider and log cabin" campaign for Harrison, declaring he felt sure the people were "too intelligent to be gulled by such trickery and flummery."

The Whig campaign of 1840 was the first rip-roaring political contest in the nation's history, cleverly planned to bury the real issues and appeal to the voters by staging great parades, festivals, and patriotic pageants that featured marchers in bright costumes, displays of caged raccoons, Indian canoes and the building of model log cabins. Although the Whigs were the party of business and property, campaign posters portrayed their candidates with shirtsleeves rolled up, hammering at a forge or following a plow, and they claimed to be more the champions of the common man than the Jacksonians had been.

Whig publicity experts, including young Horace Greeley, flooded the country with drawings, stories, song books, and jingles about Harrison's imaginary log cabin home, ignoring the fact that his real home was a stately mansion. Harrison was transformed by the politicians into a simple backwoods frontiersman, with Tyler as his faithful lieutenant. His victory over the Indians at Tippecanoe River, nearly thirty years before, was recalled with the hypnotic chant, "Tippecanoe and Tyler, too!"

In Tennessee, as elsewhere, the Whig appeal was to emotion. Polk refused to agree with a friend who wrote him that "the fact is the people like coonery and foolery better than good argument." But with their songs and chants and banners flying, the Whigs ran up some 60,000 votes in Tennessee for Harrison, against 48,000 for Van

Buren. The state Polk had fought to reclaim for the Democrats went to the Whigs, along with the rest of the nation. Van Buren and the Jacksonians were out and Harrison was President.

The defeat was a crushing one for Polk and he felt the only way he could salvage anything from it was by winning his own election for a second term as governor the following year. He wrote dozens of personal letters to Democrats throughout the state, admitting that the party had been beaten by overconfidence and "by the superior organization and industry of our opponents," but urging them not to despair. "We must take up courage," he said, "and lick the flint and try it again."

Meanwhile the sad news had come from Washington that Senator Grundy, his old law mentor and fellow Tennesseean, was dying. Polk's friends at the capital urged him to give up the race for the governorship, in which he was likely to be defeated, and appoint himself to replace Grundy in the Senate. But Polk had no intention of quitting the fight he had chosen.

Tennessee's Whigs, having learned the pattern that brought them success, made a shrewd choice in naming Polk's opponent. The man they put up against him for governor in 1841 was James C. Jones, nicknamed "Lean Jimmy" by his admiring friends. Partner in a large rope and hemp factory, owner of a big store, a former land speculator who lived in a fine brick home, Jones was offered to the voters as a "log cabin boy taken up from the plow" and he had the showmanship to put himself across as a simple-mannered, friendly, and "horny-handed farmer." Jones made the most of his personal charm and his ability to get the farmers to accept him as one of them. He complimented their wives, admired their babies, and talked their kind of talk about hunting, crops, and the weather.

His appearance fitted him for the role. Spindly tall, spare-framed, somewhat awkward, he had a solemn, almost clown-like face that made people laugh just to look at him. But the laughter was good-natured and sympathetic. Jones also had a sharp mind and if he lacked Polk's scalding wit and proven debating talent, his sense of low comedy more than made up for it. Jones realized from the start that he was no match for Polk when it came to serious argument of political issues. He decided to beat Polk at his own game of story-telling and play the jester for the crowds that came to the debates as much for entertainment and for the picnics and barbecues that followed them as they did for the sport of political warfare.

Jones simply refused to take any part in serious discussions. His ignorance of state and national affairs never embarrassed him since he made up his own facts to suit his purposes as he went along and kept repeating them in each new debate, no matter how many times Polk disproved them. Whenever Polk tried to pin him down, "Lean Jimmy" would evade the issue by clowning, by waving a piece of coon fur, or even by laughing at himself and admitting he just couldn't understand such deep arguments. He paraded his lack of "book learnin' " along with his rough appearance and slovenly dress and when Polk said he would be better suited to the circus ring than the governor's chair, Jones good-naturedly replied that they both would do well in the circus, himself as clown and Polk as "the little fellow that is dressed up in a red cap and jacket and who rides around on a pony."

Polk would have abandoned their joint debates, but

they had been taken up at his own invitation and there was no way of ending the platform contests with his clowning antagonist. By habit, Polk always dressed well, and although he could tell a good joke and enjoy one, nothing in his training or long experience in public office equipped him to meet such an opponent. Jones was for the full Whig program, for a national bank and against an independent treasury, but mostly he was for fun and games. Night and day, exhausted, suffering from colds and sometimes chills and fever, Polk went on, matching Jones hour by hour in what became an endurance contest that carried them hundreds of miles over Tennessee.

"I'm not at all discouraged at anything I see in the papers or hear from any quarter," Sarah wrote him, "but when I think of the labor and fatigue you have to undergo I feel sad and melancholy and conclude that success is not worth the labor. . . If Jones does frighten you home, you may tell him your wife will be glad to see you."

More worried than ever over his health when he was forced to give up several scheduled engagements, Sarah pleaded with him to rest. "It makes me unhappy to think what you must suffer, and for what?" she asked in another letter. "You cannot be honored by success or dishonored by defeat . . ." When the reports indicated the race definitely was turning against him, Sarah wrote, "I shall have the philosophy to stand it and think I can be as happy with my husband *at home* a defeated candidate as to have a successful one always away from me. You have now character enough in the country to stand a defeat, temporary as it must be, without injuring your future prospects. . . . If you can get through the canvass, health unimpaired, and at home safely once more, I will be content, let the result be what it may."

When the August returns were in, Polk had lost by some 3,000 votes. But he had greatly reduced the majority the Whigs had in the state during the Presidential contest the year before. Even in defeat, he had won added prestige within the Democratic party. "Polk deserves the thanks of the Democracy of the whole Union," Jackson said in a letter to Van Buren. "He fought the battle well and fought it alone." President Harrison was dead by then, Tyler had succeeded him, and despite the fact that the Whigs had taken back Tennessee, their national strength was beginning to fall apart. Polk could comfort himself with the hope, as distant as it seemed at the moment, that his ambition to become Vice President, perhaps in 1844, might not be completely lost.

As governor, he had done much to check currency inflation and reduce the state's debts, had put through many reform measures, and had given Tennessee a sound and honest administration. In his final message to the legislature he urged improved prisons and mental institutions and further corrective financial laws. Sarah and he gave a farewell party for their Nashville friends and another to which the entire membership of the legislature was invited, and he said he "might be cast down, but not destroyed" and that he cheerfully "and without complaint" yielded to the will of the people. "I retire to private life," he said. "I go to my home, the home of my early youth. . . . If I fell in the conflict, I fell with my principles, and I am proud to know that more than fifty thousand freemen, who are still unterrified and undismayed, stood by me."

Sarah and he remained in their Nashville home for another month, since builders were working on an addition to their house in Columbia. In November, they went together to visit the plantation in Mississippi, traveling in their own carriage and taking along an additional horse for riding, so Polk could enjoy a little recreation on the way. Sarah, still troubled by his poor health, tried to limit the political conferences he had with various leaders who joined them at the inns where they stayed, but she couldn't keep him from making addresses at several dinners in his honor. Still, he enjoyed the slow trip over the quiet country roads, with Sarah beside him. At the plantation in Mississippi, he rode over his lands and managed to take his mind off politics for a while.

For a time after their return home to Columbia, Polk became a gentleman of comparative leisure. He took an interest in the house and garden, in visiting with friends, dining with relatives, going with Sarah to see her folks in Murfreesboro. Retirement gave him a chance to catch up with the neglected business of the Polk estates and he made several trips to western Tennessee to sell and rent lands. He formed another of his many law partnerships and entered active practice once more, riding the circuit to earn fees by handling property claims and serving as a defense attorney in several criminal cases.

However, as the state's party chief, he spent much time in his study, writing letters, planning strategy, and furthering his own plans for the Vice Presidency. Sarah recalled in later years that there were times when she went into his study to complain that he was working too hard. Taking up a newspaper, he would quietly reply, "Sarah, here's something I wish you to read," and he would put her to work, too. Sharing his political interests, she acted as his secretary as well as his wife, but she also tried to guard his health by planning activities that would help him relax. Polk depended on her greatly for advice and always wanted her with him on the many trips he made to

Nashville for political conferences. When she objected now and then that she had household chores to finish, he would say, "Why should you stay home? Just to take care of the house? Why, if the house burns down, we can live without it."

Van Buren visited Jackson at the Hermitage in the spring of 1842 and Polk's friends did their best to get Van Buren to declare he wanted Polk to run with him as the Vice Presidential nominee in 1844. But although Van Buren said some nice things about Polk, he refused to be pinned down to a definite decision. Polk persuaded him to visit Columbia the following week and great festivities were planned to honor him in Polk's home town. The Polks gave a dinner for him and he stayed with them for the weekend, but despite the friendliness he showed Polk and the praise he gave him at public gatherings, Van Buren left without making any firm commitment about the Vice Presidency.

Polk decided it was vital for him to prove his strength in the south by making another attempt to defeat his old opponent, Governor Jones, in 1843. With that victory in his pocket, he and his friends could present a much stronger claim for the Vice Presidential nomination. Clay was almost certain to become Van Buren's rival for the Presidency and this time Polk would have everything working for him if he could defeat Jones.

The Whigs were already running up "Clay for President" banners and holding mass-meetings throughout the state. Polk announced himself as a candidate for governor and then made a quick trip to Washington to consult those working for him there. Sarah was reluctant to have him go because he had been in poor health again, but he made the journey and also went on to New York and Philadelphia to talk to Democratic leaders in those cities. Returning to Tennessee, he plunged into the contest to take Jones' place as governor.

Declaring that the people had now been given time for "sober second thoughts" after being "flagged and fiddled to their heart's content" by the Whigs, he decided to count on the "good sense of the voters" and base his campaign entirely on the issues instead of making any attempt to match the low comedy tactics Jones had used to defeat him before. Honestly believing the people were weary of hearing Jones' "old stale worn out stories," he prepared to present what he considered were convincing facts against both Jones and Clay. Polk mapped out the most grueling campaign of his career, one which would take him some 2,300 miles back and forth across Tennessee in four months, speaking an average of five hours a day. "The labor of canvassing a state like this," he pointed out in a letter to Van Buren, "from the mountains of Virginia and Carolina to the swamps of the Mississippi, is greater than can be imagined."

Sarah's letters to him, after he had been stumping only a few weeks, showed her worry. "All my fears are you cannot stand the hard labor of the canvass," she wrote. "I am not patriotic enough to make sacrifices for my country. I love myself (I mean my husband) better or more." A week later, she said, "I beg you to take care of yourself. I cannot feel happy and reconciled whilst you are undergoing so much fatigue at the risk of your health." Sending him constant political reports, helping at home to prepare and forward the information he needed in his campaign, handling the heavy load of correspondence, she wrote in May, "All I hear is good, but that does not reconcile me to a separation from you under such circumstances, since I have never wanted to see you more in my life than now." In July, she sent him a fresh supply of shirts and socks and underlined her entreaty, *"I would like to know when you are coming home?"*

But it was Jones' health that finally began to break in the ordeal, so that he lost his voice for a time. Polk wrote Sarah that despite her worry, he had never felt better in his life. His spirits were lifted by the belief that the people really were listening to his arguments, weighing the issues, and he put his trust in their judgment. Much of his time on the stump was spent denouncing Clay and the Whig policies and he revived the old charge of "bargain and corruption" that had been made when Clay helped Adams become President.

Jones accused Polk of "sticking a spear into a dead Indian" and continued his clowning and his jokes, repeating the performance that had won for him the last time. He accused Polk of wanting to use the governorship merely as a way to gain the Vice Presidency, which was a truth Polk found hard to deny. Flipping the pages of a worn copy of the *Congressional Globe,* Jones glibly invented facts it didn't contain as he pretended to "read from the record" what wasn't there. But his boldness was convincing and the Whigs controlled most of the newspapers that ridiculed Polk without mercy.

The outcome was completely uncertain when the voters went to the polls. Polk was still confident. This was one contest he *had* to win. He felt that everything he wanted depended on it. But when the count finally was completed, he was shocked and almost unbelieving. Jones had won reelection and by a larger margin than before. The Whigs had taken both houses of the legislature and swept to victory throughout the state.

Whig newspapers hailed the fact that Tennessee was a

Whig state, a national-bank state, a Clay state. Clay himself declared, "The election in Tennessee was by far the most important of the year and its successful issue more than compensates for any partial defeats we have sustained elsewhere." Considering the result decisive in his own bid for the Presidency, Clay added, "Such an event cannot fail to exert a powerful influence throughout the whole nation."

Polk bravely wrote a friend that "this is no time to indulge in a desponding feeling," but he was deeply hurt. While he had lost in Tennessee, the Democrats had made gains in other states. Van Buren wrote Polk that he thought the result "as mortifying as it is incomprehensible." Newspapers that supported Van Buren charged "Polk has not kept himself up with the progress of the Democratic party, nor with the spread of its principles," and suggested there were better candidates for the Vice Presidential nomination.

He had reached the black moment of his career. In defeat, all his hopes for the Vice Presidency seemed finally lost. What depressed him most was not only that the people of his state had twice rejected him for Jones, but that they had rejected the principles upon which he fought. From his viewpoint, they had been "fooled again" into choosing buffoonery over reason, and the result struck his deepest faith in the wisdom of the people and in the virtues of self-government.

But his own party in Tennessee was still behind him, still confident the Democrats would carry the state in the 1844 national election. Polk gradually lifted himself out of his depression. The feeling grew among many leading Democrats in other parts of the country that he had lost in Tennessee because he had supported Van Buren, who had never been popular there. They said that Polk would have won if the party had another candidate for President and that their defeat in Tennessee was a sign of sentiment among voters elsewhere in the South. Some Democratic leaders began to ask, "Will Van Buren's friends persist in running him for a third time?"

Van Buren, meanwhile, still hadn't said whom he wanted for his possible running mate. When the Democrats of Tennessee met at Nashville in November, 1843, they loyally nominated Polk for Vice President by unanimous vote, hoping they could influence the national party to think the same way. But they pointedly refused to nominate Van Buren or anyone else as their choice for President. They agreed to support whatever candidate was nominated by the coming national convention of the party in Baltimore. Polk realized he still had a chance, if only a very slim one, of winning his bid for the Vice Presidency. But it was a fighting chance and he never was a man who lacked the courage to fight for anything his heart was set on.

Chapter Ten

JAMES POLK had no idea at the start of 1844 that he soon might be President of the United States. His ambition went only as far as the Vice Presidency and he worked hard to win his party's nomination for that. It was taken for granted that the Democrats would name Van Buren for President and Polk supported him, although many party leaders in the south and southwest would have preferred some other candidate.

He was so determined to become Van Buren's running mate that he refused a post as Secretary of the Navy in President Tyler's cabinet. Polk wrote that "all the public preferment which I have at any time enjoyed, I have received directly from the hands of the people . . . and I have often declared to my friends, that if I ever again filled any public place, I expect to receive it from the same source." In a confidential letter to Cave Johnson, his friend and political manager in Washington, he explained that taking the cabinet post might prevent him from campaigning for the Vice Presidential nomination and also might be looked on as a stand against Van Buren. When Polk turned down the appointment, his former college pal John Mason was made Tyler's Navy Secretary.

Although Van Buren seemed an almost certain choice for the Presidential nomination, the Vice Presidential contest was wide open. Van Buren's backers favored running former Vice President Richard Johnson again and there were other men who had strong followings in various parts of the country. Jackson tried to help Polk by sending personal notes to some of the state leaders, suggesting that they unite behind him. But Polk faced powerful opposition and he was realistic enough to realize that the second place on the ticket wouldn't come to him easily.

His health had begun to show the effects of the long years of political battling. Sarah wasn't the only one concerned because he worked too hard and refused to relax. Others remarked that he appeared care-worn and so thin that his clothes seemed to hang upon him. As always, there were pressing family problems to add to his worries. Early in 1844, he took on the responsibility of bringing his young nephew Marshall to Columbia and acting as a father to the boy who was the son and namesake of his late brother. The boy's mother had remarried a North Carolina physician, W. C. Tate, and Polk had convinced her to put Marshall in his care.

That spring he set out on a visit to his plantation in Mississippi. While he was away, the political pot came to a sudden boil over an issue that was to change the entire course of his life, as well as that of the nation. The question of whether to annex Texas to the United States had been simmering for years, but the major parties had avoided taking sides over it since the failure of the first annexation attempt while Jackson was in the White House. Tyler had revived the issue the winter before in a message to Congress and was reported to be negotiating with Texas.

Henry Clay, who would be the Whigs' candidate for President, had called the Texas question a "freak issue" which had no place in the campaign and had taken a stand against immediate annexation. When Polk returned home from his trip to Mississippi, he made a statement that called for not only Texas, but also Oregon, to be added at once to the United States.

"Let Texas be re-annexed," he said, "and the authority and laws of the United States be established and maintained within her limits, and also the Oregon Territory, and let the fixed policy of our government be not to permit Great Britain or any other foreign power to plant a colony or hold dominion over any portion of the people or territory of either."

His use of the term "re-annexation" struck a popular note, since it played on the belief of some Americans that the United States had a legal claim to the territory dating back to the Louisiana Purchase. Polk's statement also made the most of a fear on the part of others that the British might try to take over Texas as well as Oregon. He made his position known in answer to a query about his views as a possible Vice Presidential candidate.

But what Polk didn't know at the time was that Van Buren had already written a letter, which was about to be published, that put him on record against any immediate move to annex Texas. With the Democratic convention less than a month away, Van Buren had been confident that he would be nominated, no matter what stand he took, so he had joined Clay in trying to remove the Texas issue from the campaign. Polk and many other Democrats expected Van Buren to come out in favor of Texas and they were shocked when his letter was made public. The result was that the Democratic party became hopelessly split. Its two living former Presidents, Van Buren and Jackson, were on opposite sides.

Jackson had helped make Van Buren President and he had longed to see him nominated again and re-elected, but his desire to have Texas part of the United States was stronger. Although Jackson was in poor health and in retirement at the Hermitage, he still was a powerful force in the party. Van Buren had underestimated that power in declaring himself against taking Texas into the Union. Democrats had been attacking Clay for his opposition on the same question and Van Buren stepped into the line of fire from his own party.

Quick to realize the significance of the Texas question and what he felt was the error of Van Buren's position on it, Jackson summoned Polk and several other leaders to a conference at the Hermitage. He suggested to Polk for the first time that he might be a candidate for President. Jackson told Polk that Van Buren had made a "fatal error" and that under the circumstances he never could be nominated or elected.

In a letter to Cave Johnson, in which he told about the meeting, Polk said, "I have never aspired so high and . . . in all probability the attempt to place me in the first position would be utterly abortive. . . . I aspire to the second office and should be gratified to receive the nomination." But the following day, in another letter to Johnson, Polk wrote, "He, General Jackson, thinks the candidate for the Presidency should be an annexation man and reside in the southwest, and he openly expresses (what I assure you I had never for a moment contemplated) the opinion that I would be the most available man; taking the Vice Presidential candidate from the north."

With only two weeks left before the convention, Polk

privately agreed to try to seek the Presidential nomination. He believed it was highly unlikely he would win it, but if that failed he still might be named his party's choice for second place. From his Columbia home, by letters to Washington, Polk directed the secret strategy of his campaign. He entrusted his political future to Cave Johnson and to Gideon Pillow, his law partner and close associate. With shrewd political insight he outlined the tactics they should follow.

"I have but little hope that union or harmony can be restored among the members of Congress, but I have hope that the Delegates *fresh from the people*—who are not members of Congress—and have not been so much excited can be brought together," he wrote Johnson. "Let a strong appeal be made to the delegates as fast as they come in, *to take the matter into their own hands, to control and overrule their leaders at Washington.* I suggest as a practicable plan to bring them to act—to get one Delegate from each state who may be in attendance to meet in a room at Brown's hotel. . . . If you will quietly and without announcing to the public what you are at, undertake this with energy and prosecute it with vigor, the plan is feasible, and I think it will succeed."

Johnson, Pillow, and other Polk men talked to many of the delegates as they arrived in Washington on their way to Baltimore. They let it be known that Jackson now favored Polk instead of Van Buren. Private meetings were held, strategy was discussed, but no definite plans were agreed upon. When the delegates assembled in Baltimore on May 27, 1844, a majority of them had been instructed by state conventions to vote for Van Buren. But that had been before Van Buren's anti-Texas letter was published. Many now agreed that their instructions no longer bound them. Van Buren's backers wanted the convention to choose a candidate by a simple majority vote, but the growing opposition managed to put through a rule that the choice had to be made by a two-thirds vote.

"You have more friends here than any man in the field and if your name had been brought before the Country for the *first place,* we would have far more unanimity," Pillow wrote Polk just before the balloting began. "Things may take that turn yet. We of the south cannot bring the matter up. If it should be done by the north it will all work right."

Van Buren received a majority of the votes on the first ballot, but not the necessary two-thirds. As the voting went on, his lead steadily decreased. Seven ballots were taken before the convention adjourned for the day without having selected a candidate. That evening, George Bancroft, the historian and Democratic boss of Massachusetts, helped Pillow and Johnson line up other northern delegates to offer Polk as a compromise choice.

"On this morning we brought your name before the convention for the Presidency," Pillow wrote the following day. Actually, it was not until the delegation from New Hampshire was polled on the eighth ballot that Polk received his first convention vote. New York state, on the next ballot, withdrew Van Buren's name in the interest of harmony and cast that state's votes for Polk, starting the stampede. "You received 266 votes, being every vote in the convention," Pillow continued in his letter. "Never was there such enthusiasm before seen or witnessed in any body."

Delegation after delegation had rushed to change its vote and demonstrate its loyalty to the new winner. Shouting, cheering, parading crowds created a scene common to political conventions of later years as Polk became the first "dark horse" candidate in American political history. His nomination took the country so much by surprise that when first reports of it were sent over the new telegraph lines many people thought it was a hoax. Although he had been prominent in Washington affairs, and in his own state of Tennessee, he was not as celebrated a national figure as Van Buren or Clay and in some sections of the country his name was hardly known. The Whigs made fun of the nomination by asking, "Who is James K. Polk?"

But when the news reached Clay at his home in Kentucky, the Whig leader sprang from his chair and angrily paced the room as he swore over the surprising word from Baltimore that his old enemy would now fight him for the Presidency. Along with most of the country, Clay had expected Van Buren would be his opponent. Polk's nomination would make the Texas question a live campaign issue and by tying Oregon in with it, the Democrats would have a fighting cause that would gain votes in the north as well as in the south. The party would be united behind Polk. Clay is said to have remarked, "I've been beaten again."

As Polk's running mate, the Democrats chose a northerner, George Dallas of Pennsylvania, for Vice President. The party platform set the rallying cry for the election by declaring that "our title to the whole territory of Oregon is clear and unquestionable" and that the "re-occupation of Oregon and the re-annexation of Texas at the earliest practicable period are great American measures which this convention recommends to the cordial support of the Democracy of the Union."

The Whig platform had avoided the Texas and Oregon questions. Clay later tried to modify his stand against annexing Texas in a series of campaign letters that straddled the issue, but his shifting viewpoint did him more harm than good. On another question, one of the main planks in the Whig platform was a declaration that the President should serve only a single term. Polk stole that from them right at the start of the campaign by announcing in his acceptance that he had no intention of seeking a second term.

"I deem the present to be a proper occasion to declare, that if the nomination made by the convention shall be confirmed by the people and result in my election," he said, "I shall enter upon the discharge of the high and solemn duties of the office with the settled purpose of not being a candidate for re-election."

The Democratic platform sharply criticized the political razzle-dazzle that the Whigs had indulged in during previous campaigns and called for a decision based squarely on the issues and not "in factious symbols, not in displays and appeals insulting to the judgment and subversive of the intellect of the people." However, when Whigs adopted as their mascot the raccoon which had climbed around their log cabins in 1840, the Democrats soon matched them with campaign tricks of their own. Bands of "Koon-Skinners" paraded the streets, blowing the Whig coon from a cannon's mouth and hanging the mascot in effigy as they chanted:

"Blow the trumpet, beat the drum.
Run Clay Koons. We come, we come!"

Polk's home in Columbia was deluged with letters of advice from Democrats big and small, but while he carefully considered many of the suggestions, the major campaign decisions were his own. He recognized Clay's power and brilliance and never discounted the great personal popularity of the Whig statesman. But Clay's career had been one of seeking political opportunity, swinging from one side to another, constantly changing his views to gain temporary advantage. Polk had set his course according to his Jeffersonian creed. His record was consistent and his enemies found it hard to attack him on those grounds.

He had earned the deep and bitter hatred of the Whigs for his crusade against the banks, his fight for low tariffs, his position as a leader of the Jacksonians. The fury they turned on him in the campaign became personal in its abuse. He was accused by some Whig newspapers of being a duelist, while others called him a coward afraid to defend his honor. Northern Whigs circulated shocking lies that he had mistreated slaves. Others dug far into the past to try to prove that Grandfather Ezekiel had been a Tory during the Revolution. In the south, he was denounced as a "blighted burr, fallen from the mane of the war horse of the Hermitage." Even Sarah came in for criticism from some who accused her of being a poor housekeeper who relied on servants to do things for her while she busied herself with her husband's campaign instead of tending to domestic duties. They claimed that Mrs. Clay made much better butter than Sarah Polk.

Custom did not permit Polk to take to the speaking platform on his own behalf. People would have been shocked if a candidate for the nation's highest office had gone out on his own seeking votes. Although everybody knew he wanted to be President, it would have been considered not only immodest, but also an intrusion upon the right of the voters to make up their own minds, if he had sacrificed his dignity to beg in person for their support. He wasn't supposed to appear eager for the office in any way, but merely be willing to serve if the people should choose him for the highest honor they had to bestow. A possible President was expected to be above such things as huckstering along the campaign trail. He might write letters to friends, who would then see to it that they were made public so as to express his views, or he might depend on the party's newspapers to make his opinions clear, without letting them quote him directly. But the day hadn't yet come when a candidate for President could speak in person to the people.

However, even in those days, a Presidential hopeful couldn't expect to be elected without effort. Polk directed the smallest details of the campaign from home. He chose those who were to speak for him, assigned the speakers, planned their schedules, and even arranged the buying of food for barbecues. By letter, he kept in touch with leaders in all the key states, advising them on policy, suggesting specific answers to Whig arguments, outlining the material that was to go into newspaper articles and pamphlets. He kept alert to the shifting strategy in vital areas where votes were critically needed. Dubbed "Young Hickory" by supporters who likened him to Jackson, Polk was proud of the nickname, but he soon proved he was his own man by making decisions independent even of Jackson's advice.

In July, a dinner was given in Columbia to honor the delegates who had helped nominate him at the Baltimore convention. Crowds came pouring into town, houses were illuminated, and Polk's home was besieged by well-wishers. They stood out front, cheering him while bands played, and Sarah threw open the doors to them despite the warning of friends that the mob would track mud from the road on her carpets and ruin the furniture. "The house is open to everybody," she said. Polk heartily seconded the invitation. "Let them all come in," he agreed. "They won't hurt the carpets." Sarah reported later that the crowd had "left no marks except the marks of respect."

Thousands attended a great rally in Nashville in August, where a dinner was served on "two miles of table" and the grove at Camp Hickory "fifty acres in extent, was as full as it could hold." Democratic leaders from the north and from other states miles away took turns addressing groups in various parts of the grounds because the audience was so large no speaker's voice could reach all of them at the same time.

President Tyler, long at odds with his own Whig party, had decided to run as an independent candidate and Polk's supporters were worried that he would draw Democratic votes from Polk. Learning that Tyler might consider withdrawing his candidacy if Democratic newspapers would quit attacking him and his administration, Polk speedily enlisted the aid of General Jackson in silencing the attacks. He also got others to use their influence with Tyler. Late in August, the President withdrew from the race and another barrier to Polk's election was removed.

But the bitterness of the campaign increased. One Whig pamphlet described Polk as "wholly unworthy of trust in every point of view." Another pointed to the fact that he had been twice defeated for governor of his own state and said "having no hold upon the confidence or affections of his countrymen at home, and no talent to command respect for us abroad, he is not the man for the times or the Union." Although the contest was fiercely fought in all the states, Polk began to concentrate on Tennessee and New York.

Clay forces also directed much of their fire at Tennessee. Despite Polk's eagerness to win there, Clay was to gain the victory in Tennessee by little more than a hundred votes and make Polk one of the few Presidents in history who failed to carry his own state. New York was even more important. Van Buren had rallied to Polk's aid, but the Democrats still lacked strength. Clay's shifting stand on the annexation of Texas helped them. The Whig leader had taken one position in the north and another in the south and his conflicting views lost him many northern supporters who gave their votes to abolitionist candidate James G. Birney of New York.

On election day, Polk won a plurality over Clay in New York by only five thousand votes. Throughout the nation, he gained 170 electoral votes to 105 for Clay. New York had been crucial, for if Clay had carried the state, he would have defeated Polk 141 to 134. When Jackson received the welcome news at the Hermitage that New York had gone Democratic, he dashed off a hurried victory note to Polk: " 'Who is J. K. Polk' will no longer be asked by the coons—A.J."

Many Whig newspapers, fully expecting Clay to carry New York, came out with headlines declaring Polk had been defeated and Clay was President. The news from New York was slow in reaching Tennessee, but Polk knew the election was his a full day before word reached the rest of the state. The postmaster at Cincinnati had written a note of the vote results on the outside of the package of mail from the east that reached Nashville late at night. Nashville's postmaster, a close friend of Polk's, immediately sent a special messenger to Columbia. The rider arrived at dawn and Polk was aroused from bed to learn the glad tidings.

James K. Polk was President-elect, but nobody in his home town yet knew it. For twenty-four hours, he went about his usual work, keeping the news to himself until it was confirmed. He and Sarah shared it alone and he enjoyed going to his office as usual, greeting friends he met on the street, and accepting the expressions of sympathy from many of them who thought he had been defeated. It wasn't until the next regular mail delivery arrived in Columbia a day later that the news became public and crowds gathered to cheer the new President.

Chapter Eleven

PRESIDENT-ELECT James Polk left his home in Columbia with Sarah on January 28, 1845, for Washington, determined from the beginning to hold executive leadership firmly in his own hands. He had made no pledges or commitments to the leaders of any factions of his party. "My object will be to do my duty to the country," he said in a letter to Cave Johnson. "I intend to be *myself* President of the U.S."

The fact that he was on his way to fill the nation's highest office gave him no exaggerated sense of self-importance. Like any ordinary citizen, he asked Johnson to reserve rooms for Sarah and him at Coleman's Hotel and to make sure that the rates were reasonable. "You know I have no money to spend unnecessarily," he wrote, "and to avoid being subjected to an enormous or extravagant charge it is necessary that a distinct bargain shall be made in advance."

They started the journey with an affectionate visit to the Hermitage to see Andrew Jackson, who was in such poor health both men sadly realized it might be the last time they would meet. Jackson was to die the following summer. From Nashville, the Polks went to Wheeling on a small steamer and a storm struck the Ohio River just before they reached Louisville, driving the vessel ashore among the trees. There was near panic for a time, but crew members said Polk himself calmly kept to his cabin and continued work on his papers. Although it was late at night when the boat passed Louisville, the docks were crowded with people. On Sunday, a band came aboard to play in Polk's honor, but Sarah thought it was improper to have music on the Sabbath and asked to have the musicians thanked and sent ashore. Smiling, Polk gave in to her wish and said, "Sarah directs all domestic affairs."

At Madison, Indiana, where many important guests were presented to Polk, he was most amused by an old schoolmaster who walked around him several times, stopping to study him carefully from the front, the sides, and the back, and then announcing, with a sweeping bow, "Your countenance is indicative of a broad basis." Polk made a brief speech of thanks to a throng at Cincinnati and to groups at other river landings. They traveled by carriage over the National Road from Wheeling to Cumberland, and then by railroad to Baltimore where they were met by official welcoming committees and by Vice President-elect George Dallas, whom Sarah described as "an elegant man, tall, exceedingly handsome, and gentle in manner." In the crush of people, a pickpocket tried to steal a wallet from one of Polk's traveling companions.

By the time he arrived in Washington in mid-February, he had decided he wanted Senator James Buchanan of Pennsylvania, who later was to become President himself, as his Secretary of State. But he hadn't chosen any other cabinet members. Newspapers were predicting Polk would become a mere figurehead in the hands of the politicians who would dominate the cabinet, but he quickly made it clear that he intended to be President in fact as well as name. He took the unprecedented step of drawing up a form letter to send to each prospective cabinet member, asking them to pledge themselves in advance to resign if they failed to obey the rules he set out for them.

"In making up my cabinet I desire to select gentlemen who agree with me in opinion, and who will cordially cooperate with me in carrying out these principles and policy," the letter stated. He asked them to pledge that they would take no part in disputes over who was to succeed him in office and would not interfere in matters of official patronage, that they would keep on the job and not absent themselves for long periods of time from Washington, that they would faithfully manage their offices and their staffs, and would be loyal to him and the administration. "If Sir: you concur with me in these opinions and views, I shall be pleased to have your assistance as a member of my cabinet; and now tender you the office of——," the letter said, leaving a blank space to be filled in, "and invite you to take charge of the Department."

When Polk announced the choices he had made, he showed exactly how independent he meant to be. He completely passed over Calhoun, who had been President Tyler's Secretary of State and who hoped he would be chosen to continue in that post. Despite the objections of some Democrats and most Whigs, and even against a personal plea from Jackson, Polk named Robert J. Walker of Mississippi as Secretary of the Treasury because he had confidence in his integrity and ability. For Secretary of War, he chose former New York Governor William Marcy, leader of a faction that had opposed Van Buren. Historian George Bancroft became Polk's Secretary of the Navy.

Polk's closest political friend, Cave Johnson, was Postmaster General and John Mason, his personal friend and former college classmate, was named Attorney General. Mason, who had been Tyler's Secretary of the Navy, was the only member of the former President's cabinet Polk took into his own official family. Later, after Bancroft was made Minister to England, Mason was shifted again to the Navy Secretaryship under Polk. For the confidential post of private secretary, Polk chose his nephew, J. Knox Walker.

During his term in office, Polk held more than four hundred cabinet meetings. He established regular meetings each Tuesday and Saturday and also called many special ones and created an entirely new pattern of relationship between the President and his cabinet. From it, came much of the strength that he brought to the office of the Presidency itself, so that it grew under Polk's leadership to emerge as a true executive branch of government.

Unlike most previous Presidents, and especially his Whig predecessors, who had felt duty bound to follow the decisions of the cabinet, Polk sought the advice and opinion of his cabinet members, but made his own decisions. He consulted them constantly on matters of policy, often accepted their suggestions and tried to win their approval, but he considered them only his advisers. He personally ran the administration and made final judgments himself. As master of his cabinet, he allowed no dissent from the position he finally decided to take. He encouraged all the cabinet members to share their views instead of acting separately on things that involved the various departments. When some Treasury matter came up, for example, it was discussed not only by the Secretary of the Treasury, but also by all the rest, so that he could have the full viewpoint of his entire official family. Probably more than any other President he insisted on "joint cabinet responsibility" in decisions that were made.

"I have never called for any written opinion from my cabinet," he said, "preferring to take their opinions, after discussion in cabinet and in the presence of each other. In this way, harmony of opinion is more likely to exist." He recognized that the administration could not have more than one leader and sometimes felt the need to rebuke cabinet members for trying to interfere in matters he considered none of their business. Buchanan, who was interested in promoting his own political career, caused Polk the most trouble. Several times, he reached the point of threatening to ask for Buchanan's resignation, but always managed to patch up their difficulties. Polk was particularly annoyed by Buchanan's attempt to force him, through influence in Congress, to appoint him to the Supreme Court and by his shifting views on the Oregon question.

But those problems were all in the future on March 4, 1845, when James Polk was inaugurated. It was a cheerless and rainy day and the downpour drenched not only the crowds gathered in the streets, but also the President-elect as he rode to the Capitol beside outgoing President Tyler in an open carriage drawn by four horses. The somewhat bedraggled procession was led by a chief marshal who carried ribbon-draped batons of young hickory as emblems of the new head of the republic. Taking it for granted that the weather would be fair, the arrangements committee had ordered that no carriages were to enter the Capitol grounds. Diplomats and other dignitaries had to make their way through the rain with their gaily-dressed ladies from the side gate to the scanty shelter of the portico while Polk and his escort were being received in the Senate chamber by the assembled Congress.

Sarah and her special friends watched from the gallery

while Vice President Dallas took his oath and then she hurried out to her seat on the portico, where Polk was escorted by the robed judges of the Supreme Court and by members of Congress. While the honored guests behind him stood in plumed hats that were soggy and elaborate uniforms that were damp, Sarah proudly listened to Chief Justice Taney administer the oath of office. She held in her hand something she surely didn't need on that cold and rainy day, an elaborate fan she was to keep as a proud possession all her life. Presented to her as a historic memento, it had delicately carved ivory handles and its silk cover was imprinted with portraits of all the Presidents from Washington to Polk, along with a picture of the Goddess of Liberty.

Polk at forty-nine was the youngest President ever to have taken office up to that time. His inaugural address, considered by some historians to be among the best made by any President, failed to make much of an immediate impression on the rain-soaked crowd. He had been months preparing it, rewriting it, having close friends go over it, but he read it deliberately and slowly, without any of the spirited oratory that had won him fame in the stumping contests of Tennessee. The cheers that punctuated the reading were half-hearted and old John Quincy Adams commented sourly that Polk had delivered it to "a large assemblage of umbrellas."

But in it, he made absolutely clear his position on three vital issues, the annexation of Texas, America's claims in Oregon, and the reduction of tariffs. He went even further in outlining to Bancroft, in confidence, the full program he planned for his administration. Polk told the historian he would annex Texas, would resolve the dispute over Oregon, try to acquire California, settle the tariff question in a way that would be just to both farmers and manufacturers, and that he would put an end to financial chaos and the bank controversy by establishing an independent Constitutional Treasury. In the four years of the single term to which he had pledged himself, he hoped to solve the major problems that had troubled the nation for years.

The task he set was herculean, but despite the fact that few Presidents were to meet such powerful opposition in Congress as he did, Polk methodically put through his announced plans and carried them out to the letter within the time he had allowed himself. "His administration, viewed from the standpoint of results, was perhaps the greatest in our national history, certainly one of the greatest," Bancroft was to write of him. "He succeeded because he insisted on being its center, and in overruling and guiding all his secretaries to act so as to produce unity and harmony."

With the ceremonies over, the Polks entertained a few close friends at dinner at the White House. Two inaugural balls had been planned, an elaborate one at the fashionable Carusi's Hall, to which high society had been invited at ten dollars a ticket, and a more democratic affair at five dollars a ticket, at the National Theater. Sarah, in a "mazarine blue velvet dress with a deeply fringed cape," made an appearance with him at Carusi's. When they entered and took their places on a platform at the end of the hall, dancing ceased and the band struck up *Hail to the Chief*. But after the brief reception there, the Polks went on to the National Theater and "supped with the true-blue five-dollar Democracy," as ex-President Adams put it in his diary.

Sarah did very little to renovate the White House, except for having some necessary repairs made in the public rooms. She refused the services of an expensive

New York decorating firm that suggested renovations of the Presidential quarters, saying that "if the private apartments had been satisfactory to Mrs. Tyler they would be to me." She became a busy and popular hostess, not only at constant official dinners and receptions, but to a long list of relatives, family friends, and guests who stayed at the President's Mansion.

Among the wives of the cabinet members, her closest personal friend was Mrs. Marcy. Sarah and Polk also became very fond of Dolley Madison, whose gay spirit and social prestige added much to the parties and other functions. The Polks had a good time at most of the festivities and in later years Sarah wrote, "The White House was the abode of pleasure while I was there."

Democratically, they opened the parlors two nights a week to anyone who might wish to visit the President and his Lady at home. "These informal reception evenings are very pleasant," Polk wrote in his diary. "Members of Congress, strangers and others call without ceremony and without invitation, and retire when they are disposed to do so. By setting apart two evenings in the week (Tuesdays and Fridays) I can devote the balance of the evenings of the week to business in my office." The informal gatherings usually drew fifty to a hundred people, but sometimes there was such a crowd additional parlors had to be opened and lighted. On many days, he also had guests for luncheon and for dinner and there were times when he had visitors at the breakfast table.

The Polks seldom had an opportunity to go out, however, and he complained that "my confinement to my office has been constant and unceasing." After ten months in office, he noted, "Mrs. Polk and myself dined today with the Secretary of the Navy, being the first time we have dined out since I was President." Because of his work, they were forced to turn down most invitations to social affairs outside the White House. They attended a few balls and now and then he made a personal appearance at a trade convention or some other event, but he was rarely seen by the general public. Sometimes he did step out to the White House grounds when the Marine Band performed.

Polk posed for portraits, painted by George Peter Healy and several other artists, including one made at the request of the King of France. He also had his likeness taken for medals to be presented to the Indian tribes. But he was deeply annoyed because the portrait sittings took so much of his precious time. He was also troubled when he was forced to leave his office to attend art showings, college commencements and similar affairs, and even to visit the Navy Yard to see the testing of a new diving bell. When he was called from important business to watch a magician who was performing for White House guests, he wrote in his diary that "while Mr. Alexander exhibited his art greatly to their wonder and amusement, I was thinking more about the Oregon and other public questions that bear on my mind. . . . I thought the time unprofitably spent."

The Polks were never lonely for family. There were always young nephews or nieces staying at the White House with them and they were constantly visited by other relatives as well as by friends from Tennessee and North Carolina. Accompanied by his old college friend Secretary Mason, Polk rode over to Georgetown and entered his nephew Marshall Polk in the university, paying his tuition for the fall term. Marshall was able to get back to Washington most weekends and Polk's diary shows the companionship they shared and his deep interest in the boy's welfare. Sarah's niece Johanna Rucker also came to live with them and two nephews and another niece were guests for many weeks. Polk appointed his younger brother Bill *chargé d'affaires* at Naples and was proud of the commerical treaty he later concluded with the King of the Two Sicilies.

Sam Houston was a frequent overnight guest and Polk entertained former President Tyler several times. He also tried to patch up his old quarrel with John Quincy Adams by extending to him an indirect invitation to dine at the White House, but when Adams refused unless apologies were made in advance, Polk decided to let the matter rest. "I only thought of extending that courtesy as President of the U.S. which his age and the stations he has held seemed to make proper," he wrote. Among guests at one of his dinner parties was Mrs. Alexander Hamilton, then eighty-eight years old, whom Polk described as a "very remarkable person." He noted, "She retains her intellect and memory perfectly, and my conversation with her was highly interesting."

But more and more, he found himself burdened by the work of the Presidency and "greatly exhausted by constant confinement and labor," so that he often had to get up long before breakfast and stay at his desk late at night to accomplish what was necessary. He was forced to spend his mornings, when he wasn't holding cabinet meetings, seeing those who sought appointments. He tried to shut his office to visitors at noon each day, but seldom had an afternoon that was free from interruptions so he could write his messages and papers without distractions. Everything had to be written by hand, of course, and then hand-copied and he had very little secretarial aid. Sarah made it her job to mark newspaper articles he should read and to bring letters to his attention. She would pile things beside his chair so he could glance at them whenever he had a moment to spare.

Job seekers at first were merely an annoyance to him, but he began to resent them with bitterness as he learned to cherish each minute of his time. Some were openly rude when they didn't get the appointments they thought they deserved and others begged money when they were refused jobs. On several occasions, when he was deeply touched by the story some man or woman told him, Polk dug into his own pocket to give them a few dollars.

"The pressure upon me for office has not in any degree abated," he noted after he had been President almost a year. "It is one of the most painful of my duties to hear these applications, and especially when I have no offices to bestow." A few weeks later, he wrote, "I am ready to exclaim, will the pressure for office never cease! I have no offices to bestow without turning out better men than a large majority of those who seek their places."

Polk sometimes had to take a stand against members of his own cabinet who wanted friends appointed to positions he felt they shouldn't have. While he consulted them in making major appointments, he insisted the final decisions must be his own, whatever the political consequences. He took the same attitude with members of Congress, some of whom voted against his measures because he wouldn't name them to government positions.

"The passion for office among members of Congress is very great, if not absolutely disreputable, and greatly embarrasses the operations of the Government," he confided in his diary. "They create offices by their own votes and then seek to fill them themselves. I shall refuse to appoint them, though it be at the almost certain hazard of incurring their displeasure. I am aware that by refusing their applications I may reduce my administration to a minority in both houses of Congress, but if such be the result I shall have the high satisfaction of having discharged my duty in resisting the selfishness of members of Congress."

He tried to make it a firm rule to keep Sundays free of official business, but it was one he seldom was able to follow. While he usually managed to attend church with Sarah and some visiting niece or nephew, the rest of the day was often spent catching up with paper work or in conferences. For exercise, he made it a habit to take a brief walk every morning at sunrise and again every evening at sunset, but even on his walks he usually was joined by a waiting Congressman or by someone else who hoped to catch his ear. The same thing happened when he tried to escape the White House for a little while in his carriage. Someone nearly always accompanied him to discuss business. Polk loved to ride his horse, but was in office for months before he had a chance to take his first ride. He so seldom found the opportunity that when he did it became an event to note in his diary: "Being much wearied by my long confinement for many months, I took a ride on horseback with my Private Secretary in the evening."

Like all Presidents, he was called on to receive visiting delegations. Indian chiefs, clergymen, manufacturing agents, choral societies, missionaries, and pleaders for all sorts of charities and special interests made demands on his time. He was both amused and annoyed when diplomats made formal calls in full regalia to announce that some minor member of a royal family had given birth to a child.

Once, when a Chinese visitor remarked through an interpreter that he would be happy to tell his countrymen he had met the "King of the United States," Polk tried to set him right. "I told him that there was no king in this country, but that he had seen a citizen who had been chosen by the people to manage the government for a limited time," Polk wrote. "I am not sure that he comprehended it. . . . He afterwards called on Mrs. Polk in the parlor. I understood that he said to her, he was glad he had seen the queen."

In his task as manager of the government, Polk supervised not only all reports and activities of the executive departments, but also controlled their spending. One of his major accomplishments was in setting up what amounted to the first real budget. Before his time, each department sent an independent request to Congress for money needed and the President didn't consider himself responsible for checking or controlling the estimates or for presenting a total budget. Polk changed that by insisting that all appropriation requests be submitted to him for review, by tightly controlling the finances of each department, and by demanding that his cabinet members keep accurate and up-to-date accounts.

Feeling that it was the responsibility of the President to lead and not be led by Congress, he not only planned the legislation he wanted, but also put all the influence of his office behind it and personally managed the strategy that brought it to passage. With the view that he was responsible solely to the people, and that the executive branch was independent, he felt it was his duty to use the power of the Presidency to get members of Congress to act on the program he put before them.

He considered the passage of a low-tariff act the most important of his domestic measures. The long-standing tariff dispute between the manufacturing interests of the north and the agriculturists of the south, which had dangerously threatened to split the Union, was an issue bound to place him in the center of a heated controversy. But Polk devoted four pages of his first message to Congress to a demand for the general lowering of tariff rates. He then put Treasury Secretary Walker to work on revisions he hoped would give "fair and just protection to all the great interests of the whole Union, embracing agriculture, commerce and navigation."

Polk's task in pushing through a general tariff revision along national rather than sectional lines was not easy. Although the Democrats had a large majority in the House and a small one in the Senate, many members of his own party, especially northern Democrats, were firmly against the bill. The battle was one that went on for weeks while the capital swarmed with lobbyists for the protected interests and the Whigs warned that disaster would befall the nation if the measure passed. Daniel Webster called it "so novel, so dangerous, so vicious in its general principles and so rash" that he predicted a financial panic which would leave its victims starving in the streets.

As Polk put it, the "monopolists have not surrendered the immense advantages they possessed, and the enormous profits they derived . . . until after a fierce and mighty struggle." It was a struggle won mostly by his own effort. He called key members of Congress to his office and made it clear to them that he felt not only the public good, but also the whole power and success of his administration might hang upon their votes. When one Senator, whose vote was desperately needed, decided to set out for home before the close of the session, Polk had him brought back from the railroad station. He was pained and saddened when his college friend William Haywood, then a Senator from North Carolina, resigned his seat in the Senate in a dramatic attempt to defeat the bill. Rumors that agents for the manufacturers had tried to buy the votes of other Senators shocked and disgusted him. But against all his enemies, and even some of his friends, he led the measure to success.

The passage, which was by only one vote in the Senate, resolved the dispute in a way that lasted until nearly the Civil War years and brought into operation what later was acknowledged as one of the soundest tariff acts the country had known. Instead of the panic predicted by Webster, the nation prospered. The people were well-satisfied and Polk had disposed of a dangerous issue and cleared the way for other vital legislation.

Even before it passed, he was urging Congress to act on another of the national problems he had determined to solve during his administration. There had been chaotic financial confusion over the government's banking policies ever since Polk had helped Jackson kill the privately-controlled national bank. Van Buren had fought to establish a government treasury to hold the nation's money, but the Whigs had struck it down.

Within seven weeks after he took office, Polk was working on a bill to create an independent Constitutional Treasury, but it wasn't brought up for action for nearly a year. The Whigs and the interests that had supported Biddle's defunct bank rallied their forces against it. Their denunciations of Polk were almost as bitter and as personally abusive as when he had been leading the fight against the old bank in Congress. But he succeeded in putting it through. Before long, a building with fireproof vaults, to be called the Treasury of the United States, was being constructed. The confusion that had gone on from Jackson's days was ended.

All during the successful battles for his domestic programs, Polk faced even greater troubles in foreign affairs. He was confronted right at the start of his administration with the dispute over Oregon that had been coming to a crisis for thirty years, and with the annexation of Texas and the conflicts growing out of it that pushed the nation into war. A weary and exhausted man, who had taken so much of the government on his own shoulders that he literally had begun working himself to death, he still looked with the vision of his youth toward America's new frontiers.

Chapter Twelve

WHEN JAMES POLK became President, he inherited two major quarrels with foreign governments from former President Tyler. The United States was at odds with Mexico over Texas and with Great Britain over Oregon. Polk forced both issues to a showdown and a settlement, by calling the British bluff over Oregon and by a war with Mexico, and as a result he expanded America's frontiers more than any President had since Jefferson purchased Louisiana.

Even before he occupied the White House, Polk's election, after the stand he had taken on Texas, helped influence Congress to pass a resolution inviting Texas to become a state of the Union. Three days before Polk took office, President Tyler signed the resolution and sent Andrew Jackson Donelson to Texas as an American agent to work out the arrangements. Tyler had failed the summer before in an attempt to get the Senate to agree to a formal treaty of annexation. The Congressional resolution was a compromise between the House and the Senate. Under it, the President could choose whether to act on the simple resolution inviting Texas to join the United States, or whether to try again to negotiate a formal treaty. It was expected that the decision would be left up to Polk after his inauguration, but Tyler had acted on it immediately.

When Polk became President, he had to decide whether to complete what Tyler had started. He knew there was little chance that any formal treaty with Texas would receive the necessary two-thirds vote of the Senate. This meant that the move already underway was the only practical means of achieving his campaign promise. There were disturbing reports that the British and French were doing all they could to keep Texas from annexing itself to the United States. When the Mexican minister in Washington broke off diplomatic relations and openly threatened war if Polk went through with the plan, Polk answered that it was too late to raise the question of annexation which had been "irrevocably decided."

He sent Governor Archibald Yell of Arkansas as a special messenger to tell Donelson to carry through the agreement and to urge the Texans to accept the resolution without seeking a formal treaty since that would hold up the annexation. Sam Houston preferred a treaty so that Texas might have something to say about the terms under which it joined the Union, but he finally gave in. By December 29, 1845, less than a year after his inauguration, Polk had achieved his objective. Texas was the twenty-eighth of the United States.

In his inaugural address, Polk declared that "our title to the country of the Oregon is clear and unquestionable." But he didn't mention the boundary which had been set forth in the Democratic party platform and had been part of the campaign cry of "54-40 or fight!" That extreme demand for all of Oregon, as opposed to a reasonable settlement of the northwestern boundary problem which had been pending for years, put Polk in a difficult position. Although he had the common sense to realize that some compromise would have to be reached, he had to find a way around the die-hards of his own party and also show the British that the country meant to enforce its claims.

Both nations claimed title to all the territory west of the Rocky Mountains from the northern border of California to the southern border of Alaska on the basis of early explorations, concessions by Spain and France, and by reason of settlement. Earlier agreements had opened the country to both the English and the Americans, with a provision that the treaty could be ended on one year's notice by either Britain or the United States. The debates over Oregon which had gone on in Congress for years had grown to a storm under President Tyler's administration. Demands had been made again for building forts along the route to Oregon and for granting more land to American settlers. Strong words had been used and Britain warned that passage of the resolution would mean war. Tyler had offered to compromise by setting the boundary along the 49th parallel, but the British had done nothing about it.

If Polk backed away from the extreme demand for the whole of Oregon, he would be accused of deserting his party's platform. If he insisted on it, he faced possible war with England at the same time that trouble with Mexico was threatening. Despite the British sword-rattling, Polk sent an able minister, Louis Mc Lane, to London to see what could be done. Lord Aberdeen, the British foreign secretary, seemed willing to negotiate and asked the United States to suggest terms for settlement.

Polk found himself "embarrassed, if not committed," by Tyler's offer of the 49th parallel. He instructed Secretary of State Buchanan to set out the full claims of the

United States, but to propose that the Oregon country be divided at the 49th parallel and to allow the British free ports on the part of Vancouver Island south of the line. In the interests of peace, he hoped for a quick settlement, but the British minister in Washington, Richard Pakenham, rejected the offer without even referring it to his superiors in London.

Deciding then "the only way to treat John Bull was to look him right in the eye," Polk dictated a strong note in which he withdrew the offer and told Buchanan to "assert and enforce our right to the whole of the Oregon territory." When Buchanan cautiously wanted to delay sending it, Polk insisted on its immediate transmission. "Let the proposition be absolutely withdrawn," he told his Secretary, "and then let the British minister take his own course."

The British minister, under pressure from London, approached Buchanan with a note in which he tried to make up for his earlier abruptness, but he asked that it be considered unofficial. Polk suspected Pakenham was trying to sound him out without being held to the terms of the note. "I will not exhibit our hand to him in any such way," Polk said. "Let him make it officially and then we will answer it." When Buchanan urged Polk to tread easily, he refused and wrote in his diary that Buchanan "has been from the beginning too timid."

Polk had little fear that England really would go to war over Oregon because the English wanted a settlement. Futhermore, they were involved in serious troubles with France and facing a threatened uprising in famine-stricken Ireland. In an uncompromising message to Congress, he called for taking all of Oregon and recommended that notice be given to end the existing treaty. Finally convinced that the President meant business, the

British suggested having some neutral nation arbitrate the dispute. Polk instantly rejected arbitration because he said it would be admitting the British claim to Oregon was as good as that of the United States.

Congress passed the bill to give notice of ending the treaty. House military and naval committees began to consider the nation's military defenses and Polk declared "it is better to fight for the first inch of national territory than for the last." But while he was calling the British bluff by making warlike gestures, he worked through diplomatic channels to let it be known that if the British offered a settlement on the basis of the 49th parallel, he would feel bound to submit it to Congress and let Congress make the decision.

Lord Aberdeen responded quickly. He offered to settle for the 49th parallel that his minister had so brusquely rejected, with the reservation that British settlers and the Hudson's Bay Company be allowed to keep their titles to lands they held south of the line, even though they would be subject to the laws of the United States. Polk had forced the issue to a showdown and he put it before the Senate for a decision. The Senate, by a vote of 38 to 12, advised acceptance. By his firm stand, Polk had won recognition of American territorial rights, and established a fair boundary that left no serious quarrels with our northern neighbors. He had added to the nation the land that later became the states of Oregon, Washington, Idaho and parts of Montana and Wyoming.

His difficulties with Buchanan were a constant trial to him. "Mr. Buchanan is a man of talents and is fully competent to discharge the high duties of Secretary of State, but it is one of his weaknesses (and perhaps all great men have such) that he takes on and magnifies small matters into great and undeserved importance," he wrote.

Buchanan also troubled him by making constant requests for jobs for his friends. Their differences over the Oregon question were what led Polk to start keeping the careful diary of his Presidential years, the day-to-day journal which became one of the most complete records of any President's term in the White House and a rich source of information for future historians. "I have every day since noted whatever occurred that I deemed of interest," he wrote, explaining that he wanted to have a written record "for the purpose of retaining it more distinctly in my memory."

But Polk's cabinet members gave him less trouble over patronage than members of Congress. Day after day, he complained of being "harassed and annoyed" by Congressmen "either seeking petty appointments for their friends or complaining of appointments I had made." He said the favor-seeking Congressmen threatened "the balance of power between the two great parties of the country" and that he had counted "at least twenty members of the present Congress" who had turned against him because he wouldn't hand out jobs to their friends "and in all cases I have observed that they have afterwards voted against the measures which I have recommended." Although he had a nominal majority of Democrats in both houses, he found himself "in truth in a minority in each house" because of "the disappointments about office among members, and the premature contest which they are waging in favour of their favorites for the Presidency in 1848." Declaring himself sickened with "the want of patriotism that seems to control votes," Polk said, "If I am not sustained by Congress I will fearlessly appeal to the people."

The undiminished stream of other visitors seeking jobs also continued to plague him. "Some of them were my old customers who had made frequent calls upon me for more than a year past," he wrote. Many of them he described as "a set of loafers without merit," and said, "I find as long as I treat them civilly, I shall never get clear of them." He learned to give them "very prompt and flat denials," but felt that "neither ice nor fire" would stop them.

"I cannot refuse to give audience to my fellow citizens who call upon me," he wrote. "I have been occupied three or four hours every day hearing the speeches and representations of the office seekers and their friends. I have pushed them off and fought them off with both hands like a man fighting fire. It has all been in vain. I cannot, without insulting them, refuse to see Senators and Representatives who call in behalf of their constituents. I am often exceedingly disgusted with the scenes which occur in my office."

When the story of how he loaned a hundred dollars to a Congressman who died a few days later in an alcoholic stupor was printed in the papers, he was besieged by a new army of people begging money from him. Many, to his surprise, were well-dressed women seeking handouts for husbands who had come to Washington hoping for government jobs. "I am compelled to decline," he said. "Otherwise I should be utterly bankrupt. The idea seems to prevail with many persons that the President is from his position compelled to contribute to every loafer who applies."

He smoked pipes of peace with some visiting chiefs of Indian tribes, took part in the ceremonies to launch the building of the Smithsonian Institution, and was fascinated by the visit of the celebrated midget Tom Thumb. But he had little patience with a clergyman who came to the White House to criticize him for giving army posts to several Catholic priests. "I told him that, thank God, under our Constitution there was no connection between church and state, and that in my action as President of the U.S. I recognized no distinction of creeds in my appointments to office," he said. "I have great veneration and regard for religion and sincere piety, but a hypocrite or bigoted fanatic without reason I cannot bear."

Among other visitors he did not respect was Andrew Johnson, who would be President himself one day but was then a Representative from his home state of Tennessee. As a loyal Democrat, Johnson professed to be a supporter of Polk's administration, but he had sided with the opposition on several vital measures. Polk surprised him by revealing that he had kept a careful account of his actions and accused him to his face of trying to take one position with the voters at home and another in Washington. He noted in his diary that while Johnson left his office "subdued in tone" and "denying that he was opposed to me or my administration," he would almost prefer to have a Whig in Congress in Johnson's place.

In August, 1846, Polk took his first brief vacation from Washington, the only time he had left the city since becoming President except for a single day's trip he had made to Mount Vernon the spring before. Accompanied by Sarah, their niece Johanna Rucker, and several other relatives who had been visiting the White House, he boarded a steamer for an excursion down the Potomac and the Chesapeake Bay to Fortress Monroe at Old Point Comfort, Virginia. A wind came up and the bay grew so rough that the ladies of the party became ill, although he escaped sea sickness himself. They reached the fort early the next day and had a four-room cottage near the beach, but Polk didn't get much relaxation.

After only a few hours' sleep, he was awakened by the

firing of the fort's guns in salute to him and the playing of a military band. He also had to receive the courtesy calls of the post's commandant and the officers. Summer vacationers from the nearby resort area then descended upon the cottage and he had visitors most of the day. At sunset, he was invited to inspect the defenses of the seventy-acre fortress and then the band played again at night while several hundred people prowled outside the cottage and gave him no privacy.

The next morning, a vessel arrived to take him on a visit to the Navy Yard at nearby Portsmouth, but it was met on the way by a boat from Norfolk with a delegation on board to invite him to that city. Polk explained that "after close confinement to my office for nearly eighteen months I had sought only a few days of recreation; that I was not on a tour of ceremony, and desired no parade or public attention" and he begged them to excuse him. But they insisted and he finally agreed to spend what he hoped would be an informal half-hour there.

At the Navy Yard, he was saluted by another round of booming gunfire, taken aboard a battleship, examined the dry dock, and then had to walk a considerable distance "through a broiling sun, it being one of the hottest days of the season," to the commodore's home for refreshments. There was another long walk back to the steamer that took him to Norfolk and then parades, salutes, and ceremonies. The ladies of the party were provided with carriages, but Polk "at the request of the mayor," walked on foot, "surrounded by a dense crowd of citizens and preceded by the military" to the hotel that was almost a mile from the wharf.

Nearly crushed by the waiting crowd, he spent more than an hour shaking hands. "I made an effort and endured," he wrote, "though it was anything but pleasant to me." For an hour and a half more, he waited to be taken in to dinner. Then he marched back to the boat and finally was able to escape for the return to Fortress Monroe where he "heartily rejoiced to get into my quarters where I could have some repose and rest." But the military band came to play once more in front of the cottage and rockets were set off next to it during a fireworks display. "I spent a restless and uncomfortable night," he wrote, "sleeping but little."

In the morning, he felt sick to his stomach and his legs were sore and aching. He tried to refuse visitors, but people arrived whom he felt obliged to greet. At a dinner that afternoon, he was able to "sit at the table, but eat nothing." He wanted to quit the vacation and get back to the Capitol, but he had to attend still another reception and then a storm came up which prevented the steamer from leaving. Instead of going directly to Washington, he had to take a vessel to Richmond. It was pouring rain and people there wanted him to spend the day parading, but he declined, took the first train he could get, and was glad to be back at work in his own office the following morning, even though he was half-sick and exhausted. When he opened the doors right after breakfast, there were job seekers waiting as usual.

On his fifty-first birthday, November 2, 1846, he wrote, "The last year has been one of great anxiety and labor to me." Even Christmas Day found Polk at his desk as usual, too busy to attend church with the family. The house was filled with visiting relatives, but he "remained in my office, attended to some of the business on my table, and wrote a rough draft of a message which I have made up my mind to send to Congress." Very often, he had to give up his daily walks because there was no time for them, and the horseback rides he longed to enjoy became even more infrequent as the problems of the war with Mexico settled upon him.

"I have an excellent saddle horse, and have been much in the habit of taking exercise on horseback all my life, but have been so incessantly engaged in the onerous and responsible duties of my office for many months past that I have no time to take such exercise," he noted. On January 28, 1847, he commented that it had been exactly two years since he had left his home in Columbia to take up the Presidency and added, "In truth, though I occupy a very high position, I am the hardest working man in the country."

Chapter Thirteen

MEXICO WAS openly threatening war to regain Texas when Polk became President and there were reports that the Mexicans were concentrating troops for an invasion. He moved American forces into position to occupy the area and declared that from the moment annexation was decided he would regard Texas as part of the Union. "All questions of Constitutional power to defend and protect her by driving an invading Mexican army out of her territory will be at an end," he said, "and our land and naval forces will be under orders to do so."
River, but as an independent republic Texas had claimed

But he went a step farther and brought upon himself the lasting condemnation of the Whigs and their charge that he forced the United States into war. The boundary of Texas was in dispute. When Texas had been a Mexican province its borders extended only to the Nueces the territory to the Rio Grande. When Congress adopted the resolution for annexing Texas, the boundary was left undecided, to be negotiated between Mexico and the United States. But with Mexico reportedly threatening an invasion to recover the disputed territory and possibly all of Texas, Polk took the step for which the Whigs condemned him and ordered American troops all the way to the Rio Grande. He made it clear that Mexican military posts were not to be molested, pending the outcome of negotiations, but also gave orders that if the Mexicans attacked they were to be driven out.

Polk hoped at first that by a show of force he could bring Mexico to terms without war, not only on the Texas question but also in a way that would settle outstanding debt claims against Mexico and allow for the peaceful purchase of New Mexico and California. He was determined, however, to keep Texas and gain the other territories even if war became necessary.

Although Mexico had broken off diplomatic relations, he made every effort to restore them. The same ship which took the Mexican minister back to his country also carried a secret agent of the United States, with instructions from Polk to try to convince Mexican officials that America wanted to avoid war. The agent, William Parrot, soon sent optimistic word that Mexico would be willing to receive an envoy and that he thought the differences between the two nations might be settled quickly.

Polk lost no time in sending John Slidell, a New Orleans attorney and former Congressman, as his minister. He told Slidell to adjust a permanent boundary between Mexico and the United States and to try to buy California and New Mexico. The price, Polk said, "would be of small importance." But when Slidell reached Mexico City, the government haggled over his credentials and refused to receive him. He stayed there several months, trying to break through the diplomatic barrier and gain an audience, but the Mexicans had become stubborn and it was obvious they did not intend to negotiate.

Meanwhile, in Texas, General Zachary Taylor moved his troops to the Rio Grande and set up camp opposite the town of Matamoros, with guns pointing at the public square. When Mexican officers ordered him out, he refused to go and blockaded the river to cut off supplies to the town. Fearing war at any moment, Polk continued to press for negotiations, but they failed. Slidell returned to Washington and Polk called a cabinet meeting to consider whether to ask Congress to declare a state of war. With the exception of Bancroft, the entire cabinet favored it. Bancroft said he would, too, if Mexico started the hostilities.

The cabinet meeting adjourned at 2 P.M. Four hours later, Polk received a fateful message from General Taylor: "I regret to report that a party of dragoons, sent out by me to watch the course of the river . . . became engaged with a very large force of the enemy, and after a short affair, in which some sixteen were killed or wounded, appear to have been surrounded and compelled to surrender. . . . Hostilities may now be considered as commenced."

Polk immediately called a second meeting of the cabinet and it was agreed that a message asking for a declaration of war should be sent to Congress. "I invoke the prompt action of Congress to recognize the existence of the war," Polk said in his message. Within two hours after receiving it, the House voted 174 to 14 to authorize the President to prosecute the war. The Senate debated a day and then supported Polk by a vote of 42 to 2.

From the beginning, Polk had his eyes on the frontiers of New Mexico and California. On the day Congress declared war, another cabinet meeting was held and when Buchanan suggested that the United States should advise France and Britain that it had no territorial designs on Mexico, Polk flatly refused. He told Buchanan that war had been forced upon the United States and that in making peace we would try to "obtain California and other portions of Mexican territory" that would repay the country for the costs of war and satisfy outstanding debt claims against Mexico. Buchanan protested that unless we pledged not to take such territory the English and French might join Mexico in the war against us.

"I told him that before I would make the pledge which he proposed, I would meet the war which either England or France or all the powers of Christendom might wage and that I would stand and fight until the last man among us fell in conflict," Polk said. "I told him that neither as a citizen nor as President would I permit any intermeddling of any European Power on this continent."

Even before the war, Polk had agents working in California, since he had decided it would be "very important that the U.S. should hold military possession of California at the time peace was made." Military and naval commanders had been fully alerted to the possible outbreak of war and as soon as it was declared, Polk sent orders for them to go into action. Commodore Stockton took the port of Monterey on July 7, 1846, and a captain under his command occupied San Francisco two days later. Americans in California already had revolted against Mexican rule and they soon came under the leadership of explorer John Frémont, who joined forces with Stockton. Polk meanwhile ordered General Stephen Kearney to lead his troops across the Santa Fe Trail into New Mexico. Kearney captured Santa Fe without a struggle and went on to California.

Polk became Commander-in-Chief of the armed forces in fact as well as in title. He personally directed the grand strategy of the war, commanded his generals, issued the orders, and insisted on the final authority in all military matters. From his desk in Washington, hundreds of miles from the fighting fronts, he also tried to take charge of many local matters of tactics, in which he sometimes was less successful than he was in directing over-all strategy because of poor communications. He brought the War and Navy Departments under his direct control and with the advice of his officers and cabinet members decided that the northern provinces of Mexico were to be taken and held, and planned the action in New Mexico and California. He also decided that Mexico City itself was to be taken by a landing at Veracruz and an inward invasion from there.

At times, he felt his generals were causing him as much trouble as the enemy. His supreme command was in the hands of two generals who were Whigs and they constantly opposed his policies in order to embarrass him politically. Zachary Taylor, although a heroic commander, developed an unfounded suspicion that Polk failed to appreciate his services and began attacking the administration. Taylor's friends built up his heroism at Polk's expense to promote him as a Whig candidate for President. Winfield Scott, a man whose feelings were easily hurt, bombarded Polk with petty complaints and took it upon himself to try to make diplomatic decisions that were the President's. But much of the trouble was caused by bad communications. Letters were so delayed and telegraphic dispatches so garbled that Polk and his top generals sometimes failed to understand each other's motives clearly.

Throughout the war, Polk never gave up trying to negotiate peace. He seized every opportunity, no matter how unpromising. One such attempt led to his dealing secretly with the exiled Mexican leader, Santa Anna. Polk was led to believe by an agent of Santa Anna's that if he were again in control of Mexico, he would promptly settle the war in America's favor. Although Polk had strong doubts, he weighed them against his anxiety to end the war as soon as possible and issued orders to the American naval commander in the Gulf not to interfere with Santa Anna's attempt to make his way back to Mexico from his exile in Cuba. He was passed through the American blockade, welcomed to Mexico as a hero, and soon was in control of the country. But once in power again, Santa Anna flatly refused to negotiate. He became Mexico's ablest military commander and prolonged the war instead of shortening it.

By late September, 1846, General Taylor's forces were in possession of Monterrey, Mexico, and the first large-scale victory for the United States had been achieved. But instead of pressing on to capture the Mexican army, Taylor decided on his own authority to declare an armistice in the hope that he could get the Mexicans to talk peace. Polk immediately ordered him to cancel the truce and to hold his fortified position so troops could be drawn from his forces to aid in the planned attack on Veracruz and Mexico City. Instead, Taylor moved on toward Buena Vista, where he was in grave danger of being overwhelmed by the Mexicans.

When Taylor saved himself from the dangerous position he was in and soundly defeated the Mexican forces at Buena Vista, Polk received word of the great victory with mixed reactions. He was pleased, but still considered Taylor's action one of "great rashness." It was the last opportunity Taylor had to gain fame during the Mexican War, but it was enough to win him acclaim as a national hero and lead him to the White House in the next election.

Polk had already started to put his campaign for the capture of Mexico City into operation. The account in his diary of one of the cabinet meetings at which it was discussed shows how carefully he plotted the detailed strategy: "I next brought up the plan of conducting the war . . . and suggested the importance of taking Veracruz by a land force to be landed out of reach of the fortress, who could invest the town of Veracruz in the rear and cooperate with the blockading squadron by sea, and submitted whether by these means the Fortress of San Juan de Ulloa would not be compelled to surrender for want of supplies in a very few days. I suggested further that if this could be done the fortress after surrendering could be dismantled and blown up and that our troop on land might then march into the City of Mexico."

He ordered an advance on Tampico, had diagrams made of Veracruz and the surrounding country and drew plans for the landing and capture of the port. After Veracruz had been taken, Polk personally took charge of making sure General Scott had enough troops under his command to continue the march to Mexico City. The first landing was made at Veracruz in March, 1847, and six months later Polk's initial plans for the capture of Mexico City were completed.

In the spring of 1847 he decided to assign someone to the army in Mexico with authority to negotiate a treaty with the Mexicans when they were ready to seek peace. "Such is the jealousy of the different factions of the Democratic party in reference to the next Presidential Election that it is impossible to appoint any prominent man," he wrote. For that reason, he turned to the chief clerk of the State Department, Nicholas Trist, who seemed to fit the requirements. Trist had studied law under Thomas Jefferson, had married Jefferson's granddaughter, was an executor of his will and later had become a secretary to

Andrew Jackson and an American consul in Havana. He also spoke Spanish.

Polk gave him specific instructions and cautioned him about the need for absolute secrecy, but Trist was hardly on his way to Mexico before word of the mission leaked out to the newspapers. Although Polk was unable to find out for sure whether Trist was responsible, he lost some of his confidence in the man. Trist and General Scott, jealous of each other's authority, refused at first to cooperate and wouldn't even meet. They both sent petulant and complaining letters back to Polk from army headquarters and he was exasperated with them. Finally, after two months of quarreling, the two did get together, and instead of being enemies became the strongest of friends. Polk was troubled then because Trist and Scott plotted together to make a treaty with Mexico on their own terms.

Under the strain of directing not only the war and the peace efforts, but also the smallest details of each department of government which he considered it his personal duty to supervise, Polk's health began to break once more. He suffered frequent colds and stomach disorders that sometimes forced him to carry on his work from a sofa in the White House parlor. Sarah also was ill for a time, which added to his worries. During one of her severe attacks of chills and fever, Polk spent the nights at her bedside and then went on to his own day's work with little sleep. When Treasury Secretary Walker and later Secretary of War Marcy became ill, Polk added their activities to his own to make up for the lack of their services.

He refused to slow down and he expected those who served him to work just as hard. When even minor troubles developed, Polk demanded instant action to correct them. Typical was the case of a report made to him that the receiver of public funds at a government land office in a remote part of Ohio was some seven thousand dollars short in his accounts. "I ordered him to be removed instantly," Polk noted. "In less than three hours after the case was reported to me the removal was made, a commission issued for his successor, signed, and the orders issued for the U.S. Attorney for the District of Ohio to prosecute criminally the defaulting Receiver, and also to commence suit for the amount of the default against his securities."

Polk rewarded Jefferson Davis, General Taylor's son-in-law and later President of the Confederacy, by making him a brigadier general for his gallantry in battle, although it meant he had to deny the appointment to one of his closest friends. He also insisted on promoting some men from the ranks, to make lieutenants of private soldiers who had distinguished themselves in battle, despite the strong opposition of his generals who insisted that only graduates of West Point should become officers. When the army's Adjutant General was slow in providing a list of men for such appointments, Polk reminded him that under the Constitution he was Commander-in-Chief, told him to produce the list at once and to "regard what I said as a military order."

He took a vacation late in May, 1847, to attend graduation exercises at the University of North Carolina and a gala reception that had been planned for him at his alma mater. Sarah and his college classmate, Navy Secretary Mason, went with him and so did several relatives and other close friends. Met by welcoming committees, military bands, governors, and mayors all along the route, he performed the usual hand-shaking chores at railroad stations and at dinners where crowds who gathered to see the President sometimes grew to thousands.

At Raleigh, he was met by another old classmate, Professor William Green, later the first Episcopal bishop of Mississippi, and by a student committee. Green made a welcoming speech, which Polk answered, and he then went on to a great public reception at the state Capitol. Escorted by Green and the committee of students, he reached Chapel Hill the next evening, to be greeted by the university's president, faculty, and trustees. "Of all the Professors I had left at the University 29 years ago, Professor Mitchell alone remained," Polk wrote, remembering how Elisha Mitchell had so deeply influenced him as a student. "He met me most cordially and I was much gratified to see him. These ceremonies being over, I returned to the hotel where I had the pleasure to meet many old friends whom I had not seen since I graduated in June, 1818. Our meeting was delightful. Some of the incidents of our college life were at once recited."

He stayed up a good part of the night talking over old times and spent the next day walking around the campus and going through part of the village. "Many objects were perfectly familiar to me, and brought up fresh to recollection many of the scenes of my youth," he wrote. He sat in on a senior class examination on Constitutional law, heard freshmen recite memorized speeches, made an address to the Dialectic Society, and showed Sarah his old college room. On commencement day, he went out to the grounds to shake hands for several hours and congratulated each of the graduating students. Immediately after the ceremonies were over, he set out for the return trip to Raleigh. The carriage was delayed so that he and Sarah were forced to ride all night, but "there was moonlight & it was pleasant traveling."

The following month, he made a short tour of New York and New England, finally accepting invitations which he had postponed since becoming President. He visited Philadelphia, Baltimore and New York City, went on to Boston by way of Connecticut, and then to Maine. "I saw many hundreds of thousands of my fellow citizens," he wrote. "I saw a section of my country in New England which I had never before visited." Describing the tour as "an exceedingly gratifying one" and his reception everywhere as "respectful and cordial," he said he was much delighted and that "not an unpleasant incident occurred to mar its pleasure."

While he was touring the north, Sarah and her niece went to Tennessee. In a letter to her at her mother's home in Murfreesboro, he told her not to be alarmed by newspaper accounts that he was in bad health. "My health has been good, but my fatigue has been so great that I have been at some times almost worn down," he said. Sarah's reason for going to Tennessee was to measure the rooms of the Nashville home they had bought for his retirement, so she could get carpets and curtains. The house had once belonged to Felix Grundy and they were having it remodeled and looking forward expectantly to the time when they could leave Washington for good and live there.

Despite his attempt to reassure Sarah about his health, she was worried when she returned to Washington and saw how exhausted he was. Many of their friends were also concerned and some warned her if he kept on working so hard he might not live out his term. They suggested a way to get him to relax would be for her to insist that he take her out for rides in their carriage. "I did so," she said, "and the carriage waited and waited, until it was too late. It would have been obliged to wait all day, for somebody was always in the office and Mr. Polk would not, or could not, come. I seldom succeeded in getting him to drive with me."

Young Marshall Polk, who continued to spend most weekends at the White House, sorely disappointed him by failing to keep up with his studies. Polk transferred him to another school, but warned him it was his last chance. When Marshall finally managed to complete his studies, Polk appointed him a cadet at West Point. He also helped one of Grundy's grandsons, who came running to the White House one night after a quarrel with his teachers at a nearby school. Polk investigated the matter and used a little "Presidential influence" to convince the boy there was nothing to be gained by running away from things and that he should go back and face the trouble.

"I am fifty-two years old today, this being my birthday," he wrote in his diary on November 2, 1847. "I have now passed through two-thirds of my Presidential term, and most heartily wish that the remaining third was over, for I am sincerely desirous to have the enjoyment of retirement in private life." When friends urged him, as many leading Democrats frequently did, to change his mind and seek a second term, he answered that he had "no desire to continue beyond the present term and that I looked forward to the period of my retirement with sincere pleasure." He was told the party might find it necessary to renominate him and he might be chosen even without his consent and he replied that he would not accept under any circumstances. The following year, when the clamor increased, he sent a message to the party's national convention, repeating the one-term pledge he had made when he entered the White House.

Gradually some of Polk's worst political enemies came

to make their peace with him. Henry Wise of Virginia, who had led Polk's tormentors when he was Speaker of the House, came to his office to express his gratitude for being allowed to remain as minister to Brazil. Wise had been appointed to the post under President Tyler and Polk had decided not to recall him, despite their old enmity. "I learn that he returns to the U.S. my friend and his expressions of gratitude to me to-day were as strong and decided as human language could make them," Polk wrote, "so that I have lived to conquer the hostility of at least one of my political opponents and persecutors."

Next was John Bell, who had fought Polk for the Speakership and in the political wars of Tennessee. Elected to the Senate, Bell had sent friends to sound Polk out about patching up their differences. When he learned that the President held no grudge that couldn't be healed, he hurried to Polk's office. "I had not spoken to him since the contest between us for Speaker of the House," Polk wrote. "He appeared at first somewhat embarrassed, but I soon put him at ease." Polk told Bell he was glad to see him and was willing to let the past be forgotten. "He said that was his desire, that we were to live as neighbors when we retired from public life, and that he desired to be on terms of friendship." They talked for half an hour, shook hands, and arranged for Mrs. Polk and Mrs. Bell to get together.

Finally his greatest political enemy of all paid a surprise call on him. "I was informed by my porter that the Hon. Henry Clay of Kentucky, who was the opposing candidate for the Presidency when I was chosen, had called to see me and that he was in the parlour below stairs," Polk wrote in his diary on Februray 4, 1848. He hurried down and received him politely and courteously. "He said he entertained no feelings toward me of an unkind character. I at once replied that I entertained none such towards him and that I was glad to see him, and added that there was no citizen of the U.S. whom I would be more gratified to see in my parlour than himself." When Sarah joined them, Clay jokingly remarked that although there might be some difference of opinion in Washington over her husband's administration, he had heard nothing but praise for her own administration as First Lady. "There was a hearty laugh," Polk noted, "and he left in an excellent humor." After that, Clay came to dinner with them and was a guest at several White House receptions.

Meanwhile the negotiations with Mexico had become Polk's biggest problem. Trist had met with the Mexicans and found them unwilling at first to sign any treaty which would grant the United States a boundary that reached to the Rio Grande. Despite his firm instructions to accept nothing less than that, he had agreed to submit a Mexican offer to Washington. Polk decided to recall Trist from Mexico because he had failed in his mission and exceeded his authority by suggesting terms "which would dismember the state of Texas."

Before the orders recalling him reached Trist, however, Mexico City had fallen and the fighting was all but over. Believing that the orders were issued before the government was aware of the changed military situation and that he might now be able to get a treaty on the terms in his original instructions, Trist decided to ignore the recall, stay in Mexico City, and make another attempt to negotiate for peace. Polk and the cabinet naturally were outraged by Trist's defiance. Calling it "arrogant, impudent, and very insulting to his government and even personally offensive to the President," Polk said, "He admits he is acting without authority and in violation of the positive order recalling him. . . . He has acted worse than any man in the public employ whom I have ever known."

With the military victory won, Buchanan and Treasury Secretary Walker were backing a demand shared by many Americans that the United States should keep the whole of Mexico. Polk was against that, but he felt the country had been in a position to dictate strong terms and that Trist had greatly weakened that position. However, since Trist already was conducting the negotiations that he had taken upon himself, Polk finally decided that he would not automatically reject any treaty Trist might sign, but would decide only after he had learned what was in it.

On February 18, 1848, Polk wrote in his diary: "About 2 o'clock P.M. Mr. Buchanan called and brought with him a Telegraphic dispatch which he had just received, dated at Charleston, S.C., to-day. It was in cipher. The figures had been confused in the transmission and there was great difficulty in deciphering it. As well as could be made out it was from Mr. Trist, though his name was not signed to it, announcing that he had arrived at Charleston from Mexico, with a treaty that had been signed and ratified. It is not certain that this is the precise substance, but it is the best that can be made of the cipher." Two days later, the Treaty of Guadalupe Hidalgo was received. Polk studied it carefully, submitted it to his cabinet, and finally called a meeting to announce that he had decided to send the treaty to the Senate.

He said his decision was based on the fact that the treaty called for the boundary that was set in Trist's original instructions and that although "if the treaty was now to be made, I should demand more territory," it was doubtful that Mexico would consent to more than Trist had agreed upon. "If I were now to reject a Treaty made upon my own terms, as authorized in April last . . . the probability is that Congress would not grant either men or money to prosecute the war." As a result, he might be compelled to withdraw American troops "and thus lose the two Provinces of New Mexico & Upper California."

Buchanan and Walker were strongly against submitting the treaty to the Senate, but the rest of the cabinet approved. Polk reminded Buchanan that he previously had opposed taking any Mexican territory and now was arguing that we should take all of Mexico. "He wished to throw the whole responsibility on me of sending the treaty to the Senate," Polk noted in his diary. "If it was received well by the country, being a member of my administration he would not be injured by it in his Presidential aspirations . . . if, on the other hand, it should not be received well, he could say, 'I advised against it.' "

Polk accepted that responsibility and was preparing his message to accompany the treaty when John Quincy Adams suffered a stroke at his seat in the House. Adams was carried unconscious to the Speaker's Room and both houses of Congress adjourned. The next day, Polk sent his message and the treaty to the Senate, but the messenger returned with it. The Senate had adjourned again, out of respect to Adams, who remained in the Speaker's Room at the Capitol, where he was dying. When death came to the elderly ex-President, all business was halted. Polk closed government offices and ordered a period of mourning. Even the momentous news of the treaty was delayed and the Senate didn't really get down to work on it until after Adams' funeral.

Senate acceptance seemed doubtful. Polk called influential Senators to his office and urged them to support it, held daily conferences on it for weeks, reasoned with members of the Foreign Relations Committee who wanted to reject it on the grounds that Trist had drafted the treaty after his recall. Those who were against having the United States gain any territory at all from the war and those who wanted to take all of Mexico had joined forces to defeat the ratification. "Extremes sometimes meet and act effectively for negative purposes, but never for affirmative purposes," Polk noted. But as he counted the probable votes he won for it day by day, he became more confident that his battle to put it through would succeed. On March 10, the Senate finally ratified it, by a vote of 38 to 14, four Senators not voting.

Polk capped his victory by persuading Chairman Ambrose Sevier of the Foreign Relations Committee to resign from the Senate and take the treaty to Mexico to secure that country's ratification. Several important changes had been made in the treaty and it was far from certain Mexico would approve. But the commissioners accomplished their mission and Polk received word early in June that the treaty had been ratified by Mexico on May 25.

The winter before, Polk had selected the site for the Washington Monument "on the Bank of the Potomac South of the canal and West of 15th Street, embracing about 30 acres of land," and he laid the cornerstone for it at a great patriotic celebration on July 4. Groups of school children, the assembled cabinet, and other dignitaries were led to the site by troops of cavalry to witness the ceremonies. Polk, on horseback, received the salute of military units drawn up along Pennsylvania Avenue. On the afternoon of that Independence Day, an envoy arrived at the White House with the ratified treaty with Mexico. Polk immediately had a proclamation drawn up, announcing officially that the war was over and the nation was at peace. Having already pushed the country's frontiers to Oregon and Texas, he had added another 500,000 square miles. July 4 being a Tuesday, the White House was opened to visitors as usual that evening. "The East Room and all the parlours were lighted up," Polk wrote in his diary. "The Marine Band attended and played south of the Mansion. I retired at a late hour exceedingly fatigued."

Chapter Fourteen

JAMES POLK's last year in the White House was not a happy one. He had achieved the goals he set for his administration, but he found himself decidedly unpopular because of his determination to "represent all the states and preserve the harmony of the Union" at a time when inflamed passions had begun to divide the north and south over slavery. The controversy that had troubled him since the start of his political life grew to a fury during the last of his term in office.

He clearly foresaw the danger to the nation that would come from the slavery conflict and his whole policy was devoted to finding a compromise which would keep the country's political parties from dividing north and south "at the hazard of disturbing the harmony if not dissolving the Union itself." He saw it as his duty as President to give "no countenance to any movement which tended to violence or the disunion of the states," and said, "I deplore the state of things; I will do all I can to correct it; I will do my duty and leave the rest to God and my country."

As a slaveholder himself, like many Presidents before him and also Zachary Taylor who succeeded him, Polk might have been expected to side entirely with the south. But although he was a southerner, he had a much stronger allegiance to the Union. Many southern Democrats were both surprised and angered to discover that Polk put what he saw as his duty to the whole country above what might have been his personal sympathies.

"I expressed my fears that the extremes of the South ... and the extremes of the North ... might unite and thus keep the subject of slavery open for political agitation," he wrote in his diary, telling of one of the discussions he had with his cabinet. "I added that I feared there were a few Southern men who had become so excited that they were indifferent to the preservation of the Union. I stated that I put my face alike against Southern agitators and Northern fanatics and should do everything in my power to allay excitement by adjusting the question of slavery and preserving the Union."

But as a moderate, with extremists on both sides gaining in power, Polk found himself caught in the middle. He sadly watched his own Democratic party split apart when the abolitionists chose Martin Van Buren as a separate Presidential candidate against regular Democrat Lewis Cass and thus made it easier for the Whigs to elect Zachary Taylor. The Whigs were unmerciful in their attempt to discredit forever everything Polk's administration had done. They charged that he had launched the Mexican War merely to make slave territories of the land that had been won. Many Democrats were as vengeful in their attacks against him because he refused to use the Presidency to promote the spread of slavery. The abuse heaped upon him from both sides all but buried Polk politically months before he left the White House and the charges made in the heat of political excitement influenced the writing of history for years to come.

Polk's health began to fail him even more as he drove himself to establish the policies of his administration before his enemies took over the Presidency. Portraits painted of him during his last year in office showed a shocking change in his physical appearance compared with those made in 1844. His face was thin, deeply crossed with lines of worry, and his eyes tired. Polk often cut his hair himself, rather than waste the time it would take a barber to do it, and its thinning white sometimes hung raggedly over the back of his stiff collar. Still comparatively young in years for a President, he had aged markedly and almost suddenly.

His strongest desire was to settle the matter of extending American government to the territory won from Mexico, in the hope that this would help quiet the slavery issue with which it was mixed up. In 1846, Representative David Wilmot of Pennsylvania had introduced an amendment to an appropriation bill to prohibit slavery in any territory to be acquired from Mexico. There was no action on it then, but Polk invited Wilmot to his office to discuss the proviso. Polk told Wilmot that he "did not desire to extend slavery" and was personally convinced "slavery could probably never exist" in the provinces of New Mexico and California. Wilmot seemed to agree for a while that his proviso should be dropped since it would only inflame feelings that would interfere with gaining the new territory. Later, however, it was introduced again and the fight over slavery went on in Congress throughout the Mexican War, to become the vital issue when it came time to set up some form of government for the lands granted under the Mexican treaty.

Polk failed in attempts to get Congress to establish territorial government for California and New Mexico and feared that the Californians might form an independent nation outside the United States. He sent an urgent message to California, declaring it part of the United States, with no legal right to set up a separate government, promising Congress would act soon, and urging the people to respect the existing authority until then.

While the fight over territorial government went on, he was faced with international problems that helped him shape what became a basic foreign policy of the United States. Confronted by constant evidence of the meddling of European powers in affairs of the American continent, Polk sent a message to Congress reaffirming the principles of the Monroe Doctrine. In a statement that was the strongest renewal of Monroe's views that any President had made or was to make for nearly fifty years, he said it was proper "to announce to the world as our settled policy that no future European colony or dominion shall with our consent be planted or established on any part of the North American continent."

He then went beyond that to establish what has been called the "Polk Doctrine." Polk declared that the United States would forbid not only any attempt to set up European colonies by force of arms, but also by diplomatic intervention, and would not permit the sale or transfer, even with the consent of the people of the area, of any territory in the New World to a European power.

It was a policy he followed in warning the British to keep hands off the Hawaiian Islands and in offering American aid to keep the Mexican province of Yucatan from becoming a colony of Spain or England. At the same time, Polk strictly enforced American neutrality in respect to established governments. When a plan was put before him to have the United States provide funds for a revolution to gain control of Cuba, he refused, saying that "as President of the U.S. I could give no countenance to such a step and could not wink at such a movement." He did make an offer to buy Cuba from Spain, and was willing to pay one hundred million dollars for it, but Spain didn't want to sell.

Polk was elated when he learned of the French Revolution of 1848, which he described in his diary as "the most important event of modern times." He hoped for the success of other revolutions to establish democratic governments and later noted that the French Revolution was already encouraging people of the German States and of Italy to demand more from their sovereigns. But when the revolutionary German Confederation at Frankfurt asked the United States to help by supplying an American naval officer to organize and command a German navy, Polk turned down the request. He also refused to let Americans interfere in a revolt in Ireland although "all my sympathies are with the oppressed and suffering people." When the revolt failed, he expressed deep regret and sent instructions to Ambassador Bancroft in London to do what he could to try to win pardons for Irish rebels who were under arrest.

When some Americans, after the Mexican War, joined a movement to make their way into Mexico, posing as "buffalo hunters," to start a revolution in Mexico's northern provinces, Polk took stern steps to put an end to that. Declaring it would be "a clear violation of our international obligations under the late treaty with Mexico and a violation of our neutrality laws as applied to all nations with which the U.S. are at peace," he considered it his "imperative duty" to take all legal measures in his power to prevent it.

He refused to continue to pay a toll to Denmark for American goods which moved on the Baltic, saying it violated international laws. In another dispute, he succeeded in negotiating a new postal treaty with England which won the United States equal status with other nations of the world. After signing it, he remarked in his diary, "My successor will be relieved of all existing questions of difficulty with Foreign Nations. . . . His situation in this respect will be very different from mine when I assumed the administration."

Finally listening to the urgent pleas made by Sarah and by friends who insisted he must do something to regain his health, he agreed to visit Bedford Springs, Pennsylvania, in the hope that the mineral waters and a brief rest there might help. Because the White House was filled as usual with relatives, Sarah felt her duties as hostess wouldn't allow her to go with him, so he went by himself, accompanied by a Navy medical officer and his "faithful with him during all his term as President.
servant, Wm. Day, a free man of colour," who had been

It was the first time in over a year that he had been more than three miles from his office and his "labours, responsibilities and anxieties" had left him "exceedingly wearied and almost prostrated," but he was unable to escape the crowds who gathered along the rail route to Cumberland, Maryland, and at stopping places on the coach road from there to the resort. At Bedford Springs, he did manage to avoid a planned public reception by arriving ahead of schedule, but people soon hurried out from the village. Evening dancing in the hotel ballroom was halted so he could shake hands with those "who from curiosity had come to see the President of the United States." The weather was so cool he had to sleep under a blanket, which he found a great relief after Washington's sultry atmosphere, and he sampled the waters of the various springs.

"The spring of greatest medicinal virtue and chiefly used is a bold, strong fountain," he wrote. "The water contains portions of magnesia & iron. . . . There are also a white sulphur springs, a Slate Spring, a very large limestone spring, and three or four other springs." He found a mountain path he could climb for exercise before breakfast, spent the days strolling about the grounds and visiting with various friends who came to the hotel, and soon reported that the "rest, mountain air and water has invigorated and improved me," although the weather had turned rainy.

There were still dispatches from Washington, papers to sign and business that couldn't wait, but for the most part his stay was relaxing. He was invited to visit nearby homes for informal dinners and attended a gathering in the village of Bedford, where he was amused to learn that another President had visited before him, George Washington having been there during the Whisky Rebellion. But the arrival from New York of a reporter whom he disliked annoyed him and he noted that "he has, no doubt, followed me to the Springs to see what new slander he can invent for his employer."

On the return trip to Washington, he stopped at Berkeley Springs, Virginia (now West Virginia), where rival hotel managements tried to involve him in a dispute over accommodations after one of them had failed to provide a carriage for him. "In the afternoon I took a bath, but could not discover that it was in any respects superior to a bath taken anywhere else," he wrote. Several gentlemen, learning about the mix-up over the carriage, offered to give up their own reservations so he might take their place. Polk declined with thanks and said that during his absence from Washington he expected "no other or greater privileges than any other citizen, and that I would take care of myself." He finally obtained a coach that got him to the railroad on time to catch the Washington-bound train the next morning.

He found his office desk piled with routine work that had been left undone during his absence. Most of his cabinet members, as well as his private secretary, soon were away on brief vacations of their own or on other business that took them from Washington and Polk had to run the entire government almost single-handed. "I have not had my full cabinet together in council since the adjournment of Congress," he noted. "I have conducted the Government without their aid. Indeed, I have become so familiar with the duties and workings of the Government, not only upon general principles, but in its most minute details, that I find but little difficulty in doing this."

But a few months later, worn down again by his endless work at routine tasks as well as by the more important matters of the administration, he commented, "The public have no idea of the constant accumulation of business requiring the President's attention. No President who performs his duty faithfully and conscientiously can have any leisure. If he entrusts the details and smaller matters to subordinates constant errors will occur. I prefer to supervise the whole operations of the Government myself rather than entrust the public business to subordinates and this makes my duties very great."

He and Sarah had little time to themselves, but when they were able to spend a few minutes relaxing together, most of his talk was about the home to which they would retire in Nashville. He began looking forward to retirement ever more eagerly. They discussed the plans for rebuilding and refurnishing the house and Sarah made trips to New York to buy things for it, frequently taking along nieces or other young people who happened to be visiting them.

Gas lighting, which still had not taken the place of oil lamps in most private homes, was installed in the White House during the last winter of Polk's administration. Sarah, more than a little annoyed over having the Executive Mansion disrupted by the work of installing gas pipes and adjusting fixtures, put her foot down when workmen started to remove a beautiful glass chandelier from the main reception room. She felt quite smug about having saved it a few weeks later when the gas lighting failed during an important reception and she was able to carry on by lighting the wax candles of the chandelier.

Polk found himself facing daily swarms of office seekers almost as numerous as during his first days in the Presidency. Desperate for a last chance to gain government jobs from him, some refused to wait for appointments and sneaked into the office when he was busy with other work. "The office of President is generally esteemed a very high and dignified position, but I really think the public would not so regard it if they could look in occasionally and observe the kind of people by whom I am often annoyed," he wrote. "This is a penance I have to pay daily. From missions abroad down to clerkships and messengers' places I am troubled."

Despite the growing rage of Whig attacks against him, Polk followed his own course, but it became more important to him than ever to make a clear statement of his policies and principles. From his viewpoint, Zachary Taylor was "wholly unqualified" for the Presidency. "Having no opinions of his own on any one public subject, foreign or domestic, he will be compelled to rely upon the designing men who will cluster around him," Polk wrote, "and will be made to reverse, so far as the Executive can reverse, the whole policy of my administration."

He began the careful preparation of the final message he would deliver to Congress, spending months on the task, going over each part of it with cabinet members and close friends, weighing every word for exact meaning. Politically, he realized it would amount to his last testament to the American people, his last chance to set forth the beliefs that had begun in his frontier childhood and had guided his whole career.

Polk gave his mornings before breakfast to it and stayed up late at night, copying, changing, condensing it so as "to reduce its length without impairing its strength" because the "danger is that it will be so long that it will not be read by the mass of the people and by none but the politicians." As he wrote, he was aware that he might not use parts of it, but noted that "if I should not have occasion to use it, it will be left among my papers at my death." He wanted to "leave my full views on record to be judged by my countrymen and posterity." When he finally finished the message, he kept all the original notes and manuscripts, put them in envelopes to preserve them, for those who might find it "interesting to refer to them in after years."

His message, taken to the Capitol by his secretary shortly before noon on December 5, 1848, to be read to both houses of Congress, dealt with every phase of his administration, detailing not only what had been accomplished, but also explaining the guiding policies he had established. What was more important historically was that in his message Polk became the first chief executive to express clearly that the President, independent of Congress, was representative of the will of the people.

The idea, of course, was nothing new. Andrew Jackson had based his fight against the bank on the grounds that he was following the will of the people, a stand long taken by other Democrats as well as by Polk. But it was his message that presented the first thorough Constitutional argument based on the separation of powers, and the independent and equal existence of each branch of government. In defending the right of Presidential veto, Polk discussed the whole relationship between the President and Congress.

His declaration of Presidential independence seemed nothing short of political heresy to the outraged Whigs who had just won the election. Polk's views opposed the whole Whig tradition that Congress was the supreme power of government and that the people should express their will only through the decisions of Congress. "The people, by the Constitution, have commanded the President, as much as they have commanded the legislative branch of the Government, to execute their will," Polk said. Declaring that the President is responsible "to the people of the whole Union, who elected him," he pointed out that members of Congress are responsible only "to the people of particular States or districts."

Polk went on to examine the structure of Congress and to give specific examples to show why it could not claim to represent the will of all the people. He said it was obvious that the vote of a Senator from a state with a very small population had just as much weight as that of a Senator from a state with great population. In the House, he said, it was possible for a bill to be passed by the combined votes of members who represented only one-fourth of the people of the United States.

"If it be said that the Representatives in the popular branch of Congress are chosen directly by the people, it is answered, the people elect the President. If both Houses represent the states and the people, so does the President. The President represents in the executive department the whole people of the United States, as each member of the legislative department represents portions of them," he said. "The executive, legislative, and judicial each constitutes a separate coordinate department of the Government, and each is independent of the others. In the performance of their respective duties under the Constitution neither can in its legitimate action control the others."

Aside from his historic declaration, his message contained an impassioned plea for tolerance and compromise on the questions of slavery and territorial government. The rich new territories promised "increased prosperity and national greatness," he said in urging the nation to rise above "internal strifes, geographical divisions, and heated contests for political power" that endangered the "harmony of the glorious Union of our confederated states—that Union which binds us together as one people, and which for sixty years has been our shield and protection against every danger."

"Ours is a great example of a prosperous and free self-governed republic, commanding the admiration and imitation of all lovers of freedom throughout the world," Polk said. "How solemn, therefore, is the duty . . . to cultivate a patriotic spirit of harmony, of good-fellowship, of compromise and mutual concession, in the administration of the incomparable system of government formed by our fathers in the midst of almost insuperable difficulties, and transmitted to us with the injunction that we should enjoy its blessings and hand it down unimpaired to those who may come after us."

But his plea went to a Congress already divided, controlled by his political enemies, at a time when a voice of moderation was not to be heard. And although Polk clearly foresaw the danger to the nation that would follow the tragedy of Civil War, he couldn't accept the fact that slavery was too great a moral problem, too deeply an emotional struggle for freedom, to be quietly buried by any compromise. He still thought he could settle it before he left office.

His great worry was that the Whigs would allow California to be lost to the United States by permitting it to become an independent country. The discovery of gold and the beginning rush of new settlers made the problem even more urgent. He suggested three methods of settling it. Polk was willing to have the Missouri Compromise extended to the Pacific, or to let the matter of slavery be decided by the territories themselves when they applied for admission as states, or to have it decided by a judicial tribunal. He also was willing to consider any other plan Congress might suggest.

When Congress offered no plan for bringing government to the territories, and seemed ready to refuse all his suggestions, he put his full support behind the proposal by his friend, Senator Stephen Douglas of Illinois, to admit California into the Union as a state rather than as a territory. This would let the people in California decide the slavery question on their own terms. He cast aside southern sympathies, knowing California probably would ban slavery, and fought to bring the area into the United States in the only way that seemed to have a chance in Congress.

Polk strongly opposed a movement by some southern Congressmen to declare themselves against the statehood bill. He conferred with its leaders, with Senators and Representatives heading other factions, used all his persuasion to have them put aside the agitation over slavery and get behind the Douglas measure. Under his leadership, "it was agreed that each member of the Cabinet would be active in seeing members of Congress and urging them to support the Bill to admit California at once as a State." He interviewed leading Whig Congressmen, as well as Democrats, saying, "I regarded the subject above mere party considerations, and wished it settled, I cared not by whose votes."

But in spite of his urging, Congress failed to act. Polk was hopeful up to the very last minute of his term in office. Even on his final day as President, he waited at the Capitol until four in the morning, then went to his hotel room and refused to undress, because Congress was still in session and might present the California statehood bill for his signature. But at 6 A.M., on March 4, 1849, when the final bills were presented to him, the one he wanted most was not among them.

However, in his hopeless fight to get Congress to act, he had sternly reminded southern Congressmen of their duty and responsibility to the Union. Some historians say that if he had encouraged southern resistance instead of appealing for moderation, secession might have come in 1849, and that the north might have permitted the south to leave the nation without a struggle and thus permanently destroy the Union.

"I am heartily rejoiced that my term is so near its close," he wrote in his diary a few weeks earlier. "I will soon cease to be a servant and will become a sovereign. As a private citizen, I will have no one but myself to serve, and will exercise a part of the sovereign power of my country. I am sure I will be happier in this condition than in the exalted station I now hold."

His last months in the White House were crowded with dinners and receptions, with both private and public gatherings, and he revealed that he had worked out a system during his years as President to relieve some of the physical ordeal of shaking hands. Telling about the New Year's Day reception, he said, "I must have shook hands with several thousand persons." When he was asked whether his arm wasn't sore, Polk explained he had found "there was a great art in shaking hands and that I could shake hands during the whole day without suffering any bad effects from it."

If a man "surrendered his arm to be shaken, by some horizontally, by others perpendicularly, and by others again with a strong grip, he could not fail to suffer severely from it," he said, "but if he would shake and not be shaken, grip and not be gripped, taking care always to squeeze the hand of his adversary as hard as he squeezed him, he suffered no inconvenience from it." Admitting that he made the explanation jokingly, he said that it nevertheless was true. "I could generally anticipate when I was to have a strong grip . . . and when I observed a strong man approaching I took advantage of him by being a little quicker than he was and seizing him by the tip of his fingers, giving him a hearty shake, and thus preventing him from getting a full grip upon me."

In a more serious moment, "reflecting on the near approach of the termination of my Presidential term and the uncertainty of life," he wrote and signed his last will and testament, making Sarah his chief beneficiary. "Mrs. Polk knew nothing of my intention to write it," he said. "I took it with me from my office to my chamber and read it to her. It was unexpected to her and she expressed some surprise."

Feeling as he did that Zachary Taylor's election was about the worst choice the country could have made, he had a dispute with Buchanan when his Secretary of State suggested the cabinet should pay a courtesy call on Taylor. "Mr. Buchanan is an able man, but he is in small matters without judgment and sometimes acts like an old maid," Polk noted. He kept his cabinet closely allied to him to the very end, insisted that they make their resignations to him rather than to Taylor. He was very pleased when Buchanan was among the cabinet members who showed their final loyalty and friendship by escorting him to the boat when he departed from Washington.

But despite his feelings against Taylor, Polk received the incoming President with "courtesy and cordiality" when he came to call at the White House on his arrival in Washington and later gave a dinner party for him. On his last day as President, Polk was in his office "at an earlier hour than usual" because he was resolved to "leave nothing undone." He accepted the resignations of his cabinet, signed Congressional bills and army promotions, and "about sunset, having cleared my table of all the business upon it, I left the President's Mansion with my family and went to the quarters previously engaged for me at Willard's Hotel."

Leaving his secretary, servants and two nieces there with Sarah, he went on to spend most of the night at the Capitol, signing last-minute bills that were passed and hoping the one for California statehood would be among them. It wasn't, but there was a bill to establish a Department of the Interior, which he reluctantly decided to approve even though he had some doubts as to whether such a department might not "draw power from the states" and extend it to the federal government.

During his time in Washington, Polk had attended religious services at Lutheran, Episcopalian, Catholic, and Baptist churches and often had gone by himself to the Methodist church. But on his last Sunday, he went with

Sarah to the Presbyterian church they most frequently attended together and affectionately took leave of the congregation.

Riding with Taylor in a carriage to the Capitol for the inaugural ceremonies the next day, he was dismayed to hear him remark that California was too distant to become a state of the Union and that it would be better if it formed an independent government of its own. "These are alarming opinions to be held by the President of the U.S.," Polk wrote in his diary. But he hoped Taylor would change his views, which he did, after he took office. "Gen'l Taylor is, I have no doubt, a well meaning old man," Polk wrote. "He is, however, uneducated, exceedingly ignorant of public affairs, and, I should judge, of very ordinary capacity."

Received with Taylor in the Senate chamber, he listened to him make his inaugural address, which he thought was poorly written and badly delivered, and watched him take the oath of office. Polk shook his hand and said, "I hope, Sir, the country may be prosperous under your administration." Accompanying the new President, he rode back to his hotel and Taylor went on to the White House. Throughout the day, hundreds of people called on Polk at the hotel to bid him farewell.

It was pouring rain, just as it had been on the day of Polk's own inauguration, when he and his family were escorted to the boat which was to start them on their long trip home.

Chapter Fifteen

JAMES POLK had worn himself out in the service of his country and was exhausted and in ill health when he began his long homeward journey. By various boats and trains, he planned to visit cities along the way to New Orleans and then up the Mississippi and Ohio Rivers to Tennessee. The trip was a "triumphal march" during which the people offered him their praise, affection and highest honors, but it also was a month-long ordeal from which he never fully recovered. Before it was over, he was almost a dying man.

In Richmond, he made a speech to the assembled legislature. Already suffering from a bad cold, he made another address to crowds gathered at Petersburg. Blazing barrels of turpentine and tar lined the shore to welcome him to North Carolina. Parading through Wilmington in an open carriage, he was greeted as a returning native by mobs so great he was hours shaking hands and had little time to sleep. At Charleston, South Carolina, suffering from the heat, he rode again in an open carriage through the cheering crowds and attended a reception given by the governor and the mayor. Bales of cotton had been stacked along the wharf fifteen feet high and festooned with patriotic decorations to honor him.

By the time he reached Savannah, where he was greeted by firing guns and rockets, he felt almost overcome with the heat, but he had to ride through the streets, attend a dinner he was too ill to enjoy, hurry to a waiting railroad car. At Macon, there was a military parade, more suppers and receptions, and he stood on his hotel balcony to speak to the mass of people below. A thunderstorm frightened his carriage horses on the way to Columbus, Georgia, and although they were halted without accident, he was badly shaken. He drove through the night in the rain and was drenched the next day as he rode through more rain to wave to people who stood lining the streets.

"Greatly wearied and worn down," he left at six in the morning for a train to Montgomery, Alabama, and felt really ill. "Though much fatigued and suffering from violent cold and cough, the effect of the exposure to which I had been subjected," he shook hundreds of hands, waited until nearly midnight to attend a public dinner, replied to the toasts made to him, and "retired at a late hour, quite unwell." A doctor was called in to treat him, but there were more receptions before he was escorted to the landing where he boarded another boat. He "hoped during the passage of the steamer to Mobile to have some rest and recover," but it stopped at landings on the way and he had to make appearances.

As the vessel approached Mobile, other steamers crowded with people were lashed to the sides of his so that the welcomers could swarm aboard. The harbor was filled with smaller boats and a U.S. revenue cutter fired its salute as he was taken ashore for day-long festivities and a theater party at night. He consulted another doctor at Mobile, dosed himself with medicines, and went on to New Orleans. Aroused at dawn by a welcoming committee, he explained that he wanted to take the first boat he could to his home in Nashville because he was ill, but a grand reception had been planned. "I found myself compelled to yield, though I did so reluctantly and against my good judgment," he noted.

Taken to breakfast, he found an elaborate meal of fish and wines set out. "All the dishes were prepared in the French style of cooking, and to one unaccustomed to it, it was difficult to tell of what they were composed," he said. Seeing nothing before him that he "deemed it safe to eat in my state of health," he quietly asked the waiter to bring him some plain corn bread and broiled ham. For four hours, he rode through the sun, watched parading military units, and covered with dust and perspiration, had only enough time to change his clothes before attending a dinner. Torch-bearing crowds lined the route to the boat.

He was hardly able to drag himself out of bed the next morning. Near Baton Rouge, another boat that had brought people out to see him overturned and he spent an anxious time until all the passengers were rescued. He was too ill to attend the planned reception there. Moving up the Mississippi, his steamer was delayed for hours by a fog. At Natchez, cannon saluted him from shore, but he was suffering severely from sharp stomach pains and couldn't take part in the formal welcoming festivities. He had to refuse invitations to visit other cities and his illness grew worse, so that he became more concerned and wrote, "It was manifest that I required rest, if not medical treatment, before I could be restored to health."

But at Memphis, the first place in his own state that he had touched after being away from Tennessee for four years, the committee insisted that he take part in the planned welcome. He won their promise to let him make it only a token appearance, but the parades and receptions lasted through the day. He boarded the steamer once more, but by the time he reached Smithland, on the Ohio River, a doctor ordered him taken from the boat to a hotel. Two other physicians were called in and they gave him medicines. He spent two days confined to bed, under medical attention, and then decided he wanted to go on to Nashville, as sick as he was. On the ship, he lay on a bed in the lounge.

Crowds jammed the docks at Nashville, cheering him ashore. Conveyed to the public square, he was addressed by his old law partner, Governor A. V. Brown. Standing in an open carriage, "though feeling scarcely able to do so," he made a brief speech. Exhausted, he sat on a hotel porch, greeting old friends for hours, and the excitement and pleasure of seeing them again lifted his spirits some. With Sarah, he drove to visit their future home, but workmen hadn't finished rebuilding it despite a promise that it would be ready for them.

The next day, "though still very feeble," he and Sarah started for Columbia to see his mother and the rest of the family. He stopped on the way at his boyhood home, "my father's residence where I was a youth, which is on the roadside six miles from Columbia," and renewed memories by greeting a number of old residents and their descendants. Given a hero's welcome to his own home town, he was led into Columbia by a citizens' committee, met by a parading band and conducted to the public square where he made a speech from the steps of the bank. Finally, he was able to go to his mother's house. Taking her in his arms, he was shocked to see how much she, too, had aged during the time he had been in Washington. But at seventy-three, she was in far better health than he was. Happily greeted by relatives and close friends who soon crowded into the house, he was sincerely glad to be home at last.

"My journey is now over and I am again at my home, in the midst of the friends of my youth and of my riper years. My political career has been run and is now closed," he wrote. "I have been much honored by my countrymen and am deeply grateful to them. . . . Though fatigued and feeble, I spent a delightful evening with my relatives and friends."

He was too ill to go out the next day. But the following morning, he walked for a few minutes in the yard. On Sunday, he went to church with Sarah and his mother, but that afternoon a doctor was called. He spent two weeks at his mother's place, trying to rest. A delegation of two hundred school children visited the house and he had to receive them. He and Sarah went to a private dinner given by old friends, but he had to leave before it was over.

Gradually, he did feel a little better. He was able to visit his friend, General Gideon Pillow, and to take walks into town and enjoy talking to people he had known all his life. When he seemed well enough, he and Sarah returned to Nashville to see how the rebuilding of the house was coming along and then made a trip to Murfreesboro to visit Sarah's mother and relatives. He went for a horseback ride with Sarah's brother. After a week in Murfreesboro, they returned to Nashville.

The house was still not finished, but they decided to move in and set about putting it in order since "two or three rooms had been fitted up so we could occupy them." Boxes of furniture, books, groceries and other things were piled in the halls in great disorder. Typically, he began supervising the work of opening the boxes, getting a gardener to clean rubbish from the yard, seeing to it that the carpenters performed their labor promptly and efficiently.

He felt that the exercise in the house and around the grounds was helping him. But it was two weeks before the furniture was comfortably arranged and he fretted over the confusion. Unpacking books in the library, he overtaxed his strength. His stomach began troubling him again and he developed a bad cold that grew worse. Still, there seemed so much to do that he wouldn't rest. He shopped around to buy a pair of horses for the carriage, straightened out a legal tangle in the property deed, spent hours putting away books and papers.

All during his trip from Washington, he had been worried about the outbreak of cholera in cities he visited. When several fatal cases were reported in Nashville, he told Sarah it might be wise if they left the city for a while and paid another visit to his mother in Columbia. On Saturday, June 2, they took a drive together into the country after breakfast to visit an old friend, Daniel Graham, and decided to leave on Monday for Columbia.

Sunday morning, when Sarah had dressed for church, she found him lying on the sofa downstairs. "I can't go to church with you today," he said. She agreed that if he didn't feel well it might be better if he rested and said she would go alone. But he called her back as she started to leave the room. "I don't want you to go," he said. "I'm too unwell. Have a fire made in my room upstairs and send for Doctor Robertson. Tell him I want company to sit with me this morning."

The doctor came and suggested that another doctor be called in. On Monday, a third physician examined him. They told Sarah he was gravely ill. Although they tried to keep their concern from him, Polk guessed he might not recover. His worry was that Sarah might have some difficulty over the estate. She protested when he started to talk to her about it, but he insisted on telling her the details of the financial arrangements he had made so that the house never could be taken away from her and so that the income from the Mississippi plantation would support her after his death.

Polk asked to have his brother-in-law, Doctor Hays, brought in. Several other medical men were called for consultation. But none could help him. He told a Presbyterian minister who visited him, "I am about to die and have not made preparation." But when his mother brought her own minister from Columbia to his bedside, Polk said he wanted to be baptized a Methodist. He recalled the camp meeting he had attended years before in Columbia, how deeply moved he had been by the preaching of John McFerrin, and he asked to have him come. With the two Presbyterian ministers at his bedside, Polk was baptized by McFerrin, receiving the rites that had been denied him as a baby in the religious controversy that had centered around him on the old Mecklenburg frontier.

His life ebbed slowly. Friends and family sat at his bedside night and day and Sarah was always close. On the afternoon of June 15, 1849, at twenty minutes to five, his breathing stopped. Without any signs of pain or struggle, James Polk quietly passed away.

In the home in which he had so much longed to be, his body lay in state. A plain silver plate on the coffin bore his name and the dates of his birth and death. At the funeral services, McFerrin used the same text that had been the subject of his sermon at the camp meeting Polk attended near Columbia in 1833. Memorial services were held in churches throughout the country. In Washington, the minister of the Presbyterian church where the Polks had worshipped delivered a eulogy. Senator Levi Woodbury spoke in Boston at a municipal ceremony of mourning.

"He never seemed to forget he sprang from the ranks of the people," Woodbury said. "Never wild, wayward or dazzling, he looked always to the practical rather than to the poetic. He added to the public domain lands broad enough to support a nation, rich enough in gold for half a world, harbors spacious enough for whole navies. He astonished Europe and carried the flag higher and wider in both hemispheres than ever before." But it was because "his ambition was more for the calm than the tempest," Woodbury said, that he was successful in managing "the vessel of state in the perils he was compelled to face."

Marcy, his Secretary of War, wrote to Sarah, "If it be true, as is often said, that sorrows are lessened by being divided, you will derive consolation from the fact that a whole nation mourns with you." But it was a nation that failed to mourn for long. By fighting all his life for the principles in which he believed, by his independence and his moderation, Polk had made himself an unpopular man.

His enemies had started to bury his name long before he died and the flaming passions that brought in the Civil War raised a clamor of other voices and a boldness of other men that helped to make him an almost "forgotten President." Whig viewpoints influenced the history books for years, so that he was either condemned or dismissed as an unimportant figure who had occupied the White House for one short term. For some eighty years, there was no real attempt to write his biography and it was nearly a century after his death before historians began to rediscover him and to declare that he had been one of the nation's great Presidents.

Buried first in the city cemetery, his body was removed

to a vault next to his Nashville home, and finally to the grounds of the state Capitol, where Sarah was laid to rest beside him in 1893. "The mortal remains of James Knox Polk are resting in the vault beneath," says the epitaph on his tomb. "By his public policy he defined, established, and extended the boundaries of his country. He planted the laws of the American Union on the shores of the Pacific. His influence and his councils tended to organize the national treasury on the principles of the Constitution, and to apply the rule of freedom to navigation, trade and industry."